ST. MARY'S COLLEGE OF EDUCATION

LIBRARY

Date Due	Date Due	Date Due
-4 MAR 1997		
21. APR 1993		
20.		
	15. OCT 2002	
19. MAY 1997	13 DEC 2004	
20. DEC 2002	10 JAN 2005	
-8 JAN 2008		

THE ROMANTIC TRADITION IN MODERN ENGLISH POETRY

THE ROMANTIC TRADITION IN MODERN ENGLISH POETRY

Rhetoric and Experience

Geoffrey Harvey
Senior Lecturer in English
Bulmershe College of Higher Education, Reading

MACMILLAN

© Geoffrey Harvey 1986

First published 1986

Published by
THE MACMILLAN PRESS LTD
Houndmills, Basingstoke, Hampshire RG21 2XS
and London
Companies and representatives
throughout the world

Printed in Hong Kong

British Library Cataloguing in Publication Data
Harvey, Geoffrey
The Romantic tradition in modern English poetry:
rhetoric and experience.
1. English poetry – 19th century – History and
criticism   2. English poetry – 20th century –
History and criticism   3. Romanticism
I. Title
821'.009'145   PR590
ISBN 0–333–40848–9

For Lynne

Contents

Preface

In writing this book I have had in mind not only the student of poetry but also the general reader, and I have tried to focus straightforwardly on those aspects of our most widely read modern poets – Thomas Hardy, John Betjeman and Philip Larkin – which make them among the most interesting representatives of a long tradition in English verse of a poetry of equipoise; a tradition revitalised by the Romantic movement and which, so far as modern poetry is concerned, has Wordsworth as its cornerstone.

In my first chapter I endeavour to define the concepts of traditionalism, Romanticism and Modernism in the context of the often confusing and heated debate among critics about the direction of modern poetry. I am also concerned, in Chapter 2, to locate the Romantic movement's reinterpretation of the poetry of equipoise in Wordsworth's poetic aesthetic – in particular in his central emphasis on the essential connection between the poet, the reader and reality (the intimate relation between rhetoric and experience) – which has influenced poets following him in this tradition. I have chosen to offer in the succeeding chapters a detailed consideration of the work of Hardy, Betjeman and Larkin, rather than that of other poets in this tradition (for instance Kipling, Edward Thomas, or Auden) because, spanning the last century and a quarter, they testify in a striking way to its survival and continuity.

This book grew out of published articles, and I have decided to retain the varied emphases of the original material, though greatly expanded and modified, because it is precisely those relatively unexplored areas of these poets' writing that point most clearly to their influence on each other and to the essentially traditional features of their verse.

I am indebted to many critics, whom I gratefully acknowledge in my notes and bibliography; but I should also like to record my thanks to my friends and colleagues in the Department of English at Bulmershe College of Higher Education and the Department of English at the University of Reading, with whom I have discussed my ideas; and thanks is due finally to the anonymous reader for my publishers who offered helpful suggestions. As ever I am deeply indebted to my family for their patient support.

Acknowledgements

The author and publishers gratefully acknowledge permission to use the following copyright-material:

The extracts from *John Betjeman's Collected Poems* are reprinted by permission of the Trustees of the Estate of the late Sir John Betjeman and John Murray (Publishers) Ltd.

The extracts from 'I Remember, I Remember', 'Wedding-Wind', 'Church Going' and 'Reasons for Attendance' are reprinted from *The Less Deceived*, by Philip Larkin, by permission of The Marvell Press. The extracts from 'Ambulances', 'A Study of Reading Habits', 'Naturally the Foundation will Bear Your Expenses', and 'Dockery and Son' are reprinted from *The Whitsun Weddings*, by Philip Larkin, by permission of Faber and Faber Ltd. The extracts from 'Annus Mirabilis', 'Livings I', 'Livings II', 'Livings III', 'Posterity' and 'High Windows' are reprinted from *High Windows*, by Philip Larkin, by permission of Faber and Faber Ltd and Farrar, Straus and Giroux, Inc., copyright © 1974 by Philip Larkin.

Permission to reprint previously published portions of this book has been generously granted by the editors of *ARIEL* and *The Dalhousie Review*.

1 Poetry of Equipoise: Tradition in Modern Verse

Whenever poets and critics discuss the concept of 'tradition' or, what often amounts to the same thing, the notion of 'Englishness' in modern poetry, the debate usually generates a good deal of heat. Defensive positions are quickly taken up, fortified by examples of poetic procedures culled from the entire range of English verse. Some modern poets employ differing conceptions of what constitutes an English tradition in order to confirm and justify their own poetic convictions. William Empson with his commitment to irony and ambiguity is an obvious instance of this natural tendency. And varying definitions of an English tradition have also been invoked by critics such as Cleanth Brooks and F. R. Leavis, for instance, to vindicate respectively their New Critical and Moralist approaches to poetry. As one might expect, arguments about the existence and the nature of a native English poetic tradition have been sharpened considerably in recent years by the deepening gulf between Modernist and post-Modernist verse. As Geoffrey Thurley remarked a decade ago,

> It has become customary over the past five years or so to distinguish at least two kinds of modern poetry. The word 'modern*ist*' is now in fairly general use to designate the heroic revolutionary art that emerged just before and just after the First World War. There is then a clear fracture between the formally experimental verse of that period, and the technical conservatism of W. H. Auden's generation and most poetry written since.[1]

1

Clearly Geoffrey Thurley sees this hiatus in traditional English poetry, as he defines it, as manifested in matters of form and technique; a view which is endorsed by poets and critics such as Donald Davie and Yvor Winters. For them the major Modernist poets, T. S. Eliot and Ezra Pound, both Americans, who drew on symbolist strategies in order to create poems of great formal complexity and density of meaning, stand outside a native English tradition, which is characterised in Donald Davie's words by 'purity of diction',[2] or what Yvor Winters describes in similar terms as a 'plain style'.[3] These critics seek to emphasise the desirability of a poetry which places a premium on syntax, and on economy of metaphor, and which offers a logical, rational discourse.

Many critics felt that Modernism had developed out of Romanticism and that it was essentially opposed to order, reason, moderation and realism. Questions about the 'Englishness' of modern poetry then are usually related, if not to the challenge of Modernism, then to the malign influence of Romanticism. William Empson, for instance, in *Seven Types of Ambiguity*, regards Romantic poetry as essentially simplistic in its treatment of complex human experience, which he argues requires for its adequate investigation something more than simply the force of personal inspiration and a deep allegiance to the life of the feelings.[4] In his view it needs a mature and disciplined employment of irony. And Empson's argument finds support from Cleanth Brooks, in *Modern Poetry and the Tradition*, who feels that Wordsworth in particular founded his poetic on the emotions rather than the intellect; while F. R. Leavis, in *New Bearings in English Poetry*, also champions a poetry composed of irony, and is suspicious of the Romantics' concern with the 'egotistical sublime'.[5] What links these critical positions is what Geoffrey Thurley has described in *The Ironic Harvest* as the 'intellectualist' stance – a common commitment to defend 'mature' poetry as opposed to immature, or subjective verse; and a conviction that the proper aim of poetry is not to communicate visionary gleams, nor to prophesy, but to offer a 'constant check upon being deceived, taken in, deluded'.[6] I have given Thurley's argument about what he takes to be the dominant modern critical response to the concept of tradition, focusing as it does on the

Romantics, in brief outline because there is some validity in his general thesis that what he terms ironic verse has held sway in English poetry in recent years. But he overstates the situation, and he is surely mistaken in his judgement that it necessarily 'dictates a very limited order of poetry'[7] – a persistent undermining of the individual poet's work by his own ironical self-scrutiny and self-knowledge. In my reading of the modern poets I intend to discuss – Thomas Hardy, John Betjeman and Philip Larkin – I simply do not find this to be the case, for each of these poets, whom I regard as 'undeceived' realists, nevertheless finds himself able to offer a fundamentally moral, emotionally varied and truthful account of reality. And, looking back to the Romantics, equally, Thurley's conviction that the 'intellectualist' stance, or ironic posture, was missing from their 'subjective rhetoric' certainly distorts Wordsworth – the Wordsworth of the Preface to *Lyrical Ballads* as well as of poems as diverse as 'The Idiot Boy', 'Tintern Abbey', or many of the sonnets. On the contrary I wish to argue that the poets under consideration represent the modern continuation of an English tradition in which there is a dynamic co-operation between the sympathetic, affirmative and the ironic, detached response to life; and moreover that the tradition they represent (including, for instance, Chaucer, Shakespeare, Wyatt, Donne and many of the Augustans), which might usefully be called the poetry of equipoise, was given a new infusion of life and vigour by Wordsworth.

As Donald Davie has reminded us, recanting his earlier mistrust of Romanticism, we are all post-Romantic.[8] But clearly when we speak of the Romantic influence on modern English verse we need to have in mind something a good deal more sensitive, flexible and comprehensive than simply rather blunt notions of 'transcendence', or the 'egotistical sublime', fundamental as these concepts undoubtedly are. While the main thrust of Romanticism which was to influence the Modernists – manifested in the prophetic impulse, the rhetorical posture, the employment of symbolism, and sheer technical bravura – gathered momentum, an alternative, 'classical', strain was developed by Wordsworth, both in his poetry and in his poetic theory. This branch of Romanticism drew its strength from traditional poetry, and essentially it was Wordsworth's revival of the poetry of equipoise that continued through the nineteenth century and has carried over into post-Modernist verse. What I am concerned to discuss, then, is at root a Wordsworthian influence on modern poetry, which is concerned not solely with moments of vision, or with matters of language or poetic technique – Donald Davie's 'purity of diction' or Yvor Winters's 'plain style' – but with the basic interrelated issues of what constitutes the appropriate subject-matter of poetry, its proper audience and its modes of communication – in other words its rhetoric.

The inadequacy of the concepts of visionary transcendence and escapist subjectivism as determining features of the distinction between Romantic and modern poetry can be readily exemplified by brief reference to the four poets I propose to consider. Wordsworth's celebration of moments of vision, which constitutes a profoundly affirmative response to the universe, is balanced by his equally determined and unequivocal emphasis, both in the Preface to *Lyrical Ballads* – one of the great manifestos of Romanticism – and in the poetry itself, on the function of the intellect; on a detached and unimpassioned scrutiny of ordinary experience. He is concerned in Thurley's phrase not to be deceived. Wordsworth's prolonged exploration of the deep ambiguity that lies at the heart of all profound human experience emerges in a complex rhetoric of sympathy and irony, which both celebrates experience and yet places it at the same time within a mature perspective. Conversely the rejection of some form of transcendence in Thurley's arch-ironist, Thomas Hardy, should by no means be taken for granted. Indeed, as his personal writings indicate and his finest poetry bears out, under pressure from the essentially Romantic impulse that lies at the centre of his verse, his existentialist philosophy can accommodate moments of vision, of meaning won from existence by the strenuous activity of his poetic will at those rare times when he feels the universe to be in some kind of equilibrium. Similar moments of spiritual illumination, though of a more traditionally religious kind, are found too in John Betjeman, whose poetry of doubt rests on a foundation of Christian faith and draws its restless energy from the perpetual tension between these two poles of experience. And it is not only in spiritual matters that this stress is in evidence, for his response to life generally is basically one of generous affirmation; but it is qualified also by a robust scepticism. Finally, Philip Larkin, in spite of his clear-sighted view of the limitations and savage ironies of modern existence, yearns for and sometimes gains moments of epiphany, of liberation from the preoccupations of the self, which are nevertheless placed within the context of a neutral and strictly hopeless universe. In short, what we discover in all these poets is a profoundly sensitive and complex response to the muddle and the drama of ordinary, everyday human life – a deliberately chosen poetic stance which focuses tenaciously on the mundane, the intransigent and sometimes frightening features of daily existence, and yet testifies with equal fidelity to those moments of transcending freedom which give life meaning – a response which includes both an affirmation of life's worthwhileness and a stubborn refusal to be deceived. Theirs is essentially a poetry of sanity, and it constitutes a tradition that includes not only Larkin and Wordsworth, but also stretches back to Chaucer.

Indeed, in his discussion of Larkin's poetry, Andrew Motion directs our attention to an English tradition of this kind. He finds it understandably difficult to define with confidence, for the sense of Englishness he admits is a 'notoriously imprecise term, but among the members of what has been called this "English line" would obviously be Cowper, Clare and Wordsworth. Many other names spring to mind (Housman, for instance), but even these few are enough to indicate an important branch of Larkin's poetic ancestry.'[9] Larkin himself, however, has a clearer sense that this tradition, of which he and Betjeman are the continuators, originates in the nineteenth century and that for poets of the modern period it is mediated primarily through Hardy. In an interview with Anthony Thwaite on the publication of his critical anthology *All What Jazz*, he put it like this:

I had in my mind a notion that there might have been what I'd call, for want of a better phrase, an English tradition coming from the nineteenth century with people like Hardy, which was interrupted partly by the Great War, when many English poets were killed off, and partly by the really tremendous impact of Yeats, whom I think of as Celtic, and Eliot, whom I think of as American.[10]

Larkin's sense that he is situated within an English tradition located in the nineteenth century, and Andrew Motion's view that Larkin also belongs to an older poetic line, are significant for the way that they encapsulate the feeling that many critics share – and which Wordsworth particularly provides – of the dislocation and yet the continuity of tradition in Romantic poetry. And in several important respects Larkin, and also Betjeman, share an affinity not only with Hardy, but, as Motion points out, with what was fresh in Wordsworth's poetry: for instance their close interest in the strangeness of the apparently normal, depending (as John Wain has noted with reference to Wordsworth and Hardy[11]) on their unique angle of vision. But more importantly, as I have indicated, they share a special awareness of the way the human spirit may respond to the pressure of ordinary experience by asserting its claim to freedom and a sense of transcendence.

Of course the concepts of 'tradition' and 'Englishness' are very involved. A poet such as Clough, for instance, whose work can be accommodated within my definition of a poetry of equipoise, felt himself that his poetry drew its strength to some extent from both the eighteenth and the nineteenth centuries, particularly from Dryden and Byron; Hardy, who admired the poetry of William Barnes, has, like Barnes himself, some affinities of poetic principle with Hopkins; while Larkin feels a degree of poetic kinship with poets as diverse as Barnes, Christina Rossetti and Wilfred Owen. I do not wish to discount these cross-currents of affinity and influence. However, as I intend to argue, the catalyst for the particular development within Romanticism which involved both a more arduous definition of equipoise as a poetic aim, and a more central role for the reader in poetic activity, was Wordsworth. And, except for the great experimental period of Modernism, this strain in Romanticism has had a more or less continuous influence on modern poetry.

The basis of the poetic aesthetic which underpins the quintessentially English tradition of equipoise I am seeking to define has been effectively described by C. K. Stead. Writing about what constitutes good poetry, he says,

> A poem may be said to exist in a triangle, the points of which are, first, the poet, second, his audience, and, third, that area of experience which we call variously 'Reality', 'Truth', or 'Nature'. Between these points run lines of tension, and depending on the time, the place, the poet, and the audience, these lines will lengthen or shorten. ... There are infinite variations, but (in so far as such a metaphor can be exact) the finest poems in any language are likely to be those which exist in an equilateral triangle, each point pulling equally in a moment of perfect tension.[12]

Essentially I am concerned to argue that Hardy, Betjeman and Larkin, more consciously and explicitly than other modern poets – both in their poetry and in their statements about their writing – attend to this fundamental aim of equalising the tension between the three points of the poetic triangle in Stead's phrase; and that this poetic aesthetic is most clearly rooted in Wordsworth, who in his Preface to *Lyrical Ballads* was the first major modern poet to articulate fully and urgently the necessity of a clear, unambiguous and trustworthy relation between the poet, his audience and reality. In addition to addressing himself to the question of 'What is a Poet?' – and proclaiming that he is essentially no different from his readers – he identified the appropriate subject of poetry as being the 'fluxes and refluxes of the mind when agitated by the great and simple affections of our natures', and he redefined the nature of poetic rhetoric by determining to employ as his basic vehicle for poetic communication ordinary discursive syntax and the true 'language of men'.[13] Allowing for variations, as Stead warns us, it should be clear that the poets who follow Wordsworth's aesthetic and who strive in their different ways to achieve this moment of 'perfect tension' between poet, audience and reality include such figures as Tennyson, Hardy, Kipling, Housman, Edward Thomas, Auden, Betjeman and Larkin. If we are seeking to define the elusive concept of 'Englishness' in modern verse, then I suggest that it lies in the individual poet's conviction that he writes within a complex set of relations existing in a state of tension – between his awareness of his own poetic integrity, his faithful attention to the facts of his own experience, both ordinary and extraordinary, and his allegiance to the claims of a clearly conceived audience.

It is significant that of all the Romantic poets Wordsworth alone should have remained a dominant if sometimes muted influence on a poetic tradition which runs through some of the major Victorians, the better Georgians and on through Auden into the work of the major poet of the Movement. But, as I have indicated, Wordsworth was by temperament, paradoxically, the most classical of the Romantic poets. And, whereas the Modernists were prone, like the later neo-Romantics such as Dylan Thomas, to the excesses of Romanticism, Hardy, Betjeman and Larkin all retain an anti-Romantic bias in their verse, expressed in their frequently almost classical restraint, their realistic attitude to the changing human environment and their emphasis on a sharable reality; and, while they still pursue the Romantic ideal of transcendence, their temper is at the same time sceptical and empirical. It is essentially Wordsworth's poetic aesthetic, then, which has provided the foundation for the most enduring tradition in modern English verse, the poetry of equipoise.

While the influence of Wordsworth on Hardy is beginning to be properly understood, it might seem at first glance surprising that I should regard Philip Larkin as occupying a place at the apex of a tradition that is rooted in Wordsworth. However, even at the specific level of the individual poem, John Press discerns Wordsworthian qualities in Larkin's 'Church Going', a poem which he mentions in conjunction with 'Tintern Abbey'. 'Larkin's poem is Wordsworthian', says Press, 'in its brooding meditation, its tentative honesty as it explores a puzzling theme and gropes towards its weighty conclusion.'[14] But 'Tintern Abbey' also offers a further clue to Larkin's affinities with Wordsworth; his attraction, both temperamental and moral, to the claims of what Wordsworth called in that poem the 'still, sad music of humanity' (1.92). On the other hand, more recently Andrew Motion and Terry Whalen have alerted us to the way Larkin's apparently sombre stoicism is qualified not only by his comic impulse, but also by his pursuit of the Wordsworthian ideal of epiphanies, his quest for moments of transcendence in poems such as 'High Windows', 'Here', 'Water', or the central poem of the 'Livings' triptych – moments of what Whalen has described as 'agnostic wonder'.[15] However, the influence of Wordsworth on Larkin, mediated very often through the poetry of Hardy, is also important in other fundamental respects. First there is the freshness and poetic integrity of Larkin's response to experience. Larkin himself emphasises the way his poems derive their basic impulse from his raw feelings about ordinary life – from what he calls 'unsorted experience',[16] which is very close to the poetic experience of Hardy and Betjeman, but which has its ultimate origins in Wordsworth's determination to investigate and record the 'fluxes and refluxes of the mind'.[17] Secondly, he is Wordsworthian in the honesty and directness with which, again like Hardy and Betjeman, he writes about whatever happens to hold his interest. Indeed, Larkin has praised Betjeman's poems for exactly this quality; for being 'exclusively about things that impress, amuse, excite, anger or attract him, and – and this is most important – once a subject has established its claim on his attention he never questions the legitimacy of his interest'.[18] Any more, one might add, than Wordsworth does in that remarkable poem 'The Idiot Boy'. David Timms, in his book *Philip Larkin*, elucidates a third aspect of this Wordsworthian dimension of Larkin's poetic ancestry when he comments on Larkin's foregoing view of Betjeman's work: 'It is surprising, perhaps, to consider that Larkin's suggestions are in the same spirit as Wordsworth's, that "poetry is the spontaneous overflow of powerful feelings".'[19] And finally one must take account of Larkin's poetic rhetoric, founded on what he has called his 'common word-usage',[20] which, once more like Hardy and Betjeman, draws its strength from Wordsworth's radical experimentation with the real 'language of men'.[21]

Larkin, then, comes at the end of a line of descent from Wordsworth, which I am concerned to give here only in brief outline. In between stand the important and popular figures of Hardy and Betjeman, poets who, although each possessing a unique vision of the world and a strikingly individual voice, were nevertheless strongly influenced by Wordsworth. Moreover, the mark of Hardy can also be seen on Betjeman's writing; and both of these poets in their turn contributed to the development of Larkin's mature verse.

Hardy's debts to Wordsworth are evident in his pursuit of moments of vision, his introspective interest in the operation of his poetic imagination, his commitment to the rural community and the particular experience of loving-kindness and human solidarity that it represented. Wordsworth's influence is also apparent in the integrity and simplicity of Hardy's detailed observation and language, and he is Wordsworthian too in his intense desire to achieve in his poetry an accommodation between his subjective impulse to gain some sense of transcendence and his absolute need of the preservation of scientific rationality. But two most important features of his poetry, which link him with both Betjeman and Larkin and identify him as an heir to Wordsworth, are, as I have mentioned, his capacity to transfigure the commonplace, and also what one might perhaps call his moral realism. He has an acute eye for human suffering, and for him, as for Wordsworth, Betjeman and Larkin, it is a positive moral force. Hardy's well-known statement in defence of his pessimism about the human condition – that it constituted only ' "questionings" in his exploration of reality' necessary as the 'first step towards the soul's betterment'[22] – is echoed approvingly by Larkin in his discussion of the function of sadness and suffering in Hardy's poetry as an essentially maturing experience. For Larkin, Hardy's writing is a 'continual imaginative celebration of what is both the truest and the most important element in life, most important in the sense of most necessary to spiritual development'.[23] Here again we find Hardy and Larkin dwelling on one of the great themes of Wordsworth – of the 'Immortality' ode, of 'Tintern Abbey' and *The Prelude*.

Like Wordsworth, Hardy depended for the raw material of his verse on the almost random experience of quotidian reality that lay within the narrow compass of his own immediate world, and on the intensity of his emotional response to it – the flood of poems that followed the death of his wife, Emma, is perhaps the most obvious instance of this process. Here again, as Donald

Davie has argued, Larkin is indebted to Hardy.[24] Indeed, Larkin himself has revealed how Hardy's absolute dependence for the subject-matter of his poetry on the material that his own life provided (which is a major source of his poetic power) helped to shape Larkin's own work as he finally cast off his chosen model, W. B. Yeats: 'When I came to Hardy it was with the sense of relief that I didn't have to try and jack myself up to a concept of poetry that lay outside my own life – this is perhaps what I felt Yeats was trying to make me do.'[25] And, as David Timms has shown, Larkin's specific debts to Hardy can be traced in the poems themselves – in the echo of language in their similar use of the word 'prinked' in 'Beeny Cliff' and 'Next Please', and the consonance of feeling in 'After a Journey' and 'Deceptions'.[26] Blake Morrison has observed how 'Church Going' seems to spring from the same agnostic feeling of awkwardness in church that Hardy experiences in 'Afternoon Service at Mellstock'.[27]

Betjeman echoes Larkin's deep admiration for Hardy, and it is not at all surprising, therefore, to discover the influence of Hardy at work not only in his remarkable facility for producing intricate metrical arrangements, as Donald Davie has noted, but in the kind of echoes that one finds in 'Dorset', for instance, which was written in imitation of Hardy's 'Friends Beyond', or in 'Hearts Together', or in Betjeman's strange celebration of Hardy in his eccentric poem 'The Heart of Thomas Hardy'.[28] However, more important than these specific debts is the similarity of relation in these poets between their visual observation and their moral rhetoric. Larkin, Betjeman's most sympathetic and perceptive critic, who praised Hardy for his directness of treatment of the physical world, finds this same quality in Betjeman – not just his 'astonishing command of detail, both visual and circumstantial',[29] but the moral rhetoric at work in the way that 'the eye leads the spirit'.[30] Larkin directs our attention to a central quality in Betjeman's verse and defines his place in the English tradition when he indicates how in Betjeman its romantic dimension is grounded in the simple values of ordinary experience: 'Betjeman is a true heir of Thomas Hardy, who found clouds, mists and mountains "unimportant beside the wear on a threshold, or the print of a hand": his poems are about the threshold, but

it and they would be nothing without the wear.'[31] Betjeman's
poetry, then, shares the essential features of the tradition I have
been describing: a positive conviction of the value of ordinary
life; a desire to write from his own experience (of his childhood,
his concern for the physical environment of our lives, or his
spiritual crises); his absolute commitment to themes, however
unlikely or quirkish, that engage his imagination; his humanistic
faith in both individualism and a greater human solidarity; his
desire for a sense of transcendence; and the directness and
dramatic urgency of his vision and his language.

Bearing in mind Larkin's often expressed admiration for
Betjeman's poetry, it is again no surprise to discover Betjeman in
the company of Wordsworth and Hardy as one of the influences
on Larkin's verse. As David Timms has observed, 'Deceptions'
evokes Betjeman; and Timms also makes a fruitful comparison
between Larkin's 'The Whitsun Weddings' and Betjeman's 'The
Metropolitan Railway', drawing attention to the remarkable
similarity of their uses of the changing, ugly urban sprawl which
makes up much of the landscape of their respective railway
journeys – 'An Odeon flashes fire / Where stood their villa by the
murmuring fir' ('The Metropolitan Railway') and 'An Odeon
went past, a cooling tower' ('The Whitsun Weddings').[32] Moreover, one might add that 'The Whitsun Weddings' and 'The
Metropolitan Railway', with their close observation of the detail
of both landscape and social milieux as the context for the
investigation of human life and emotion, are in a direct line from
Hardy's railway poems, 'The Change' and 'Midnight on the
Great Western'.

I am not primarily concerned in this book with the rather
narrow activity of tracing specific influences from poet to poet,
fascinating as this exercise might be. Rather I trust that the
foregoing remarks will suffice to suggest that Hardy, Betjeman
and Larkin are major figures in a direct line of development from
Wordsworth, and that for them, as for him, poetic aesthetic is a
corollary of social aesthetic. What is important, therefore, is the
attitudes they share, explicitly or implicitly, about the appropriate
subject of poetry, about the poet's relationship with his audience
and about poetic rhetoric.

At first sight my choice of these particular representatives from a tradition that obviously includes several more major figures may seem to be a singular one – our finest Romantic poet, a great Victorian existential poet, a late neo-Georgian, and the leading light of the Movement. But if we are to examine the essential Englishness of this tradition of equipoise then we have to free ourselves from some of these inhibiting and sometimes unhelpful and misleading umbrella terms. The possibly surprising nature of my juxtapositions is intended to illuminate the origins and the essential features of a tradition to which by common consent the other poets I have already mentioned belong. Moreover, the poets I have chosen to discuss possess a particular historical as well as purely literary significance, for they register the important points of influence and the strength of continuity in traditional English verse. Wordsworth is its cornerstone because he redefined the tension between the poet, the audience and reality, in a way that influenced all the succeeding poets in this tradition; Hardy occupies a unique position in bridging the Victorian and early modern periods, and, as Donald Davie has argued in *Thomas Hardy and British Poetry*, he is of central importance as a major influence on modern poets; Betjeman, as Larkin has pointed out, spans the changing poetic landscape from the early 1930s to the present, and has been, together with Larkin himself, primarily instrumental in redirecting contemporary verse away from the powerful effect of Modernism;[33] and finally Larkin, as the major continuator of this tradition, is quite simply the most accomplished poet writing today – as Donald Davie has put it, 'Philip Larkin is for good or ill the effective unofficial laureate of post-1945 England.'[34]

I should perhaps make clear at this stage why I have chosen to approach each of these poets from a slightly different angle. Although, as I have indicated and as the ensuing discussion of their poetry will bear out, they share an essentially moral commitment to life, a common range of attitudes and a coherent poetic aesthetic, this fact has not been accorded critical attention because, beguiled by the exclusive and limiting concepts of Romanticism, existentialism, neo-Georgianism and the Movement, critics have tended to neglect precisely those aspects of their art which illumine their contiguity. And it is these aspects that I propose to consider. Thus I emphasise the ironic, detached, intellectual quality of Wordsworth's scrutiny of experience and its importance for his poetic rhetoric. Conversely, I focus on Hardy's existential yet fundamentally Romantic transcendental-ism. Although Betjeman's verse has been highly praised by such distinguished critics and poets as Edmund Wilson, W. H. Auden and Philip Larkin, the values it embodies have been hotly disputed by recent critics, and I am concerned to indicate his position in the mainstream of traditional English poetry by attending to his urgent moral response to the processes of historical change, and to his sensitive craftsmanship. Finally, the area of Larkin's writing which has received little attention is his explicit awareness of his audience, and his view of poetry as rhetoric. Essentially, then, by focusing on dimensions of their writing which have been largely ignored, I endeavour to stress the way in which these poets draw on a common heritage of poetic values and procedures, and also to demonstrate their common commitment to their audience and their shared concern with the art of poetic rhetoric.

A central feature of the poetry of Hardy, Betjeman and Larkin which places them within the Wordsworthian tradition of moderate, tolerant, liberal humanism manifests itself in their fundamental allegiance to the value of places in human life. They share a profound awareness of the significance of topography and history (indeed, Auden coined the word 'topophilia' to describe Betjeman's obsession with places[35]). Each of these poets possesses a special sense of the importance in human experience of the interaction between the human spirit and the spirit of place. Places are magical in Wordsworth, in such poems as 'The Idiot Boy', 'Tintern Abbey' and *The Prelude*, which vividly particularise scenes in which moments of intense, almost mystical experience have been achieved. This conviction is carried over into Hardy's poetry, where the features of the Cornish landscape, for instance – the coastal scenery of 'The Voice', 'After a Journey' or 'The Phantom Horsewoman' – bear the stamp of his wife Emma's continued existence and facilitate her resurrection in his imagina-tion. In Betjeman's verse, spiritual illumination is gained on Bray Hill, looking at the sea and the moon in 'Back from Australia', or in the richly human environment of his home town in 'On Leaving Wantage 1972'. In Larkin's poetry – in poems such as 'Wedding-Wind', 'Livings' or 'Here' – moments of spiritual liberation are achieved in such varied places as a farm, a lighthouse or an East Riding beach.

However, the common concern of these poets with the benign tyranny of place is not only spiritual. It also derives from their overwhelming moral commitment to preserving and sustaining the human scale of things. Their poems are crowded with people – individuals, families, social groups – as they explore the various meanings of human interaction in poems as diverse as 'The Idiot Boy', 'During Wind and Rain', 'The Metropolitan Railway' and 'The Whitsun Weddings'. Places are fundamental to this process, for in these poems the moonlit landscape, the family home, the station buffet and the postal districts of London remain as mute but resonant witnesses to lives shaped within particular environments, which become part of the texture and meaning of ordinary lived experience. Sometimes the significance of the experience may be ambiguous, as in Wordsworth's sonnet 'Composed upon Westminster Bridge', in which the poet feels compelled to analyse the true complexity of the experience that the apparently beautiful and tranquil city offers; or powerful and particular, as in Hardy's poem 'Old Furniture', which celebrates the way simple domestic objects have been hallowed by successive generations of life-affirming activity; or intimately related to historical change, as in Betjeman's 'The Metropolitan Railway', in which he examines how ordinary people's apprehension of life's meaning is defined by the physical context of their daily routine, at the station buffet and their suburban homestead; or the deeply sustaining rituals of the rural community, as in Larkin's 'Show Saturday'.

Most important, however, for the poets of the tradition that I am describing, places incorporate a sense of communal values and foster their survival and continuity. The world of Wordsworth's and Hardy's rustics is an interdependent, caring community, which is underwritten by the familiar routines of shared experience, and a fundamental human solidarity. Conversely, the soulless modernity of the kind of atomistic society ruled by the commercial ethic that Wordsworth identifies in his sonnet 'The world is too much with us' is echoed and scorned by Hardy in 'Old Furniture', when he declares that the world has no use for someone such as he who views the ideology of progress with scepticism and distaste. Similarly, Betjeman bitterly laments the breakdown of human relationships symbolised by the urbanised and vandalised landscape of twentieth-century Britain, which in his view has fallen into the philistine hands of bureaucrats and developers, who rip the hearts out of old country towns and, as in 'The Newest Bath Guide', ignore the vital dimensions of human scale. And Larkin, who caustically describes Britain in 'Going, Going' as 'the first slum of Europe', demonstrates in poems such as 'Here', 'Sunny Prestatyn' or 'Mr Bleaney' great compassion for people whose search for happiness in the modern world seems doomed to failure in the bleak cityscapes of materialism.

These poets, although liberal and compassionate, are thus also conservative in the profoundest sense. Wordsworth's allegiance in his sonnet 'The world is too much with us' to the vital myths of Proteus and Triton, as opposed to the enervating, materialistic rhythms of 'Getting and spending'; Hardy's defence of simple rural experience; Betjeman's ardent commitment to the preservation not merely of old buildings, but of the communities and values they represent; and Larkin's disgust at urbanisation, cheap stores and foul-smelling highways – all add up to a tradition of profoundly instinctual conservatism. They all fear the moral, social and aesthetic breakdown that politically manipulated commercialism and bureaucratically organised collectivism alike threaten. This is far from being a naïve, sentimental romanticism, a retreat into the myths of pastoralism, or simple snobbish elitism. It is a desperate conservatism born of deep, imaginative compassion. This is why a poet so alert to the dangers of nostalgia as Larkin is pays reverent tribute to rituals which sustain a sense of continuity, solidarity and worthwhileness in ordinary life, whether familial or social, as in 'To the Sea' or 'Show Saturday'; just as Betjeman does in 'Autumn 1964'; or like Hardy in 'During Wind and Rain'. And the underlying impulse of their poetry is perhaps best summarised in Larkin's statement

I write poems to preserve things I have seen/thought/felt (if I may so indicate a composite and complex experience) both for myself and for others, though I feel that my prime responsibility is to the experience itself, which I am trying to keep from oblivion for its own sake. Why I should do this I have no idea, but I think the impulse to preserve lies at the bottom of all art.[36]

Their poetic aesthetic is the corollary of their social aesthetic.

The final major aspect of these poets' writing which unites them in the same tradition and sets them at odds particularly with the Modernist philosophy and its poetic aesthetic is quite simply their popularity. The immense appeal that these poets enjoy for the ordinary reader of poetry springs directly from their conscious preoccupation with the claims of their audience. Indeed, Graham Hough has identified this as an important aspect of traditional poetry:

I believe that a poet's traditional quality, though it may be displayed and expounded by historical scholarship, actually realises itself in his relation to his readers, and in his relation to a certain community of human feeling – what Johnson called the 'uniformity of sentiment' that underwrites poetic communication.[37]

Hough's view of the importance of the 'common reader' has been dismissed more recently by Neil Powell on the grounds that

It has very little to do with literary criticism, and indeed it confuses his critical standards: discontent with the audience may act as a catalyst in a literary revolution, and there is plenty of evidence to suggest that this happened in the case of modernism; but a complacent unprofessional audience is only likely to encourage – if it encourages anything at all complacent unprofessional poetry.[38]

But there is no obvious reason why Hough's 'certain community of human feeling' has to be equated with a 'complacent unprofessional audience'. And does Neil Powell really mean that an ideal audience is one that is composed only of other poets and literary critics? This view is certainly very close to that of T. S. Eliot, who wrote, 'It is wrong of Mr. Kipling to address a large audience; but it is a better thing than to address a small one. The only better thing is to address the one hypothetical Intelligent Man who does not exist and who is the audience of the artist.'[39] It is striking and instructive to juxtapose Eliot's statement, which was echoed by Ezra Pound and represents the Modernist view, with this one of Larkin's, which can stand for the poets of the English tradition:

> It is not sufficient to say that poetry has lost its audience, and so need no longer consider it: lots of people still read and even buy poetry. More accurately, poetry has lost its old audience and gained a new one. . . . In short, the modern poetic audience . . . is a *student* audience, pure and simple. At first sight this may not seem a bad thing. . . . But at bottom poetry, like all art, is inextricably bound up with giving pleasure, and if a poet loses his pleasure-seeking audience he has lost the only audience worth having, for which the dutiful mob that signs on every September is no substitute.[40]

Larkin's fundamental quarrel with Modernism, which turns its back on the pleasure-seeking audience, is therefore very much to do with its poetic rhetoric, for its 'definitive characteristic', he has said, 'was an obscurity unlike previous types in being deliberate and unnecessary'.[41] Eliot's notion of an exclusive audience certainly had its effect on his poetic rhetoric, with its density of literary allusion, its symbolic complexity and sheer difficulty for the reader; and Larkin uses Eliot as a touchstone for defining one aspect of his admiration for Betjeman's poetry as a continuation of the English tradition – for Betjeman, he says, 'there has been no symbolism, no objective correlative, no T. S. Eliot or Ezra Pound'.[42]

In the poets of the English tradition, then, and particularly those that I am concerned with, coexisting with a profoundly conservative instinct is a radically democratising approach to the communication of poetry. It is rooted in Wordsworth, who asserts in his Preface to *Lyrical Ballads* that the poet inhabits and experiences the same world as his readers and in much the same way that they do. In the passage in which he discusses 'What is a Poet?' he is quite explicit that the poet is different from the reader only in the degree of his sympathies and his capacity to employ language; and he goes on to argue that a poet's business is to move the reader's feelings, discipline his thoughts and energise his moral being – and that this can only be achieved through the employment of the normal syntactical structures and familiar language of ordinary speech. And it is precisely this kind of commitment to their audience and to the art of poetic communication that have made Hardy, Betjeman and Larkin our most widely read serious modern poets. However, they have all fallen foul of critics who, influenced by high Romanticism or Modernism, seek vainly in their writing for elevated language, for allusiveness, symbolic density, or a bardic strain. Like Wordsworth's *Lyrical Ballads*, Hardy's poems have been persistently undervalued on the grounds of their subject-matter and bluntness of tone; and in addition for their use of colloquialisms, archaisms and coinages. Betjeman too has been castigated for his seemingly whimsical playing with tone, his comic zest and his adoption of bourgeois subjects and language. And Larkin's jokiness, and his occasional employment of coarse colloquialisms have been regarded by some critics as lapses from high poetic seriousness.

As I hope the following chapters will show, these critical misjudgements occur because of a basic misunderstanding of the tradition within which these poets are writing, a tradition which involves a romantic commitment to the exploration of some sense of transcendence counterbalanced by a classical restraint and a refusal to be deceived by the vagaries and complexities of experience. This essentially English interplay and mutual qualification of the romantic and classical tempers implies, and indeed requires, a rhetoric composed fundamentally of sympathy and irony – sympathy drawing the reader into the world of the poem; irony preserving at the same time a necessary detachment and intellectual scrutiny of experience. In Wordsworth this involves a careful counterpointing of imagery and syntax, which can be observed at work within various poetic forms; while in Hardy there is a similar though more elusive process operating, which incorporates not only narrative structures and *personae*, but also imagistic sequences and ballad refrains, in a tactful but pervasive pattern of commitment and withdrawal. Betjeman's rhetoric employs a wider use of the counterbalancing of tragic nuance with slyly ironic comedy, of romantic image with worldy wisdom. And, in many of Larkin's most impressive poems, the common ground between poet and reader is established by means of a special kind of rhetoric implicit in shared embarrassment, as his *personae* produce a tension in the reader between the impulse towards identification, on the one hand, and towards retreat and sceptical evaluation, on the other.

These rhetorical strategies all demand a particularly conscious and scrupulous employment of the elements of poetic form. Yet the strength of these poets derives not, as in the case of the Modernists, from the energy and excitement of their formal experiments, but from their moral realism and their allegiance to the world of their readers. Paradoxically, as Larkin has pointed out, they display remarkably little concern with form as such:

> The poetry I've enjoyed has been the kind of poetry you'd associate with me – Hardy pre-eminently, Wilfred Owen, Auden, Christina Rossetti, William Barnes; on the whole people to whom technique seems to matter less than content, people who accept the forms they have inherited but use them to express their own content.[43]

The poets I am concerned with are all conservative poets in this sense. They all rely on traditional forms such as the ballad, the lyric, the sonnet or the dramatic monologue. However, as Larkin implies, they put these old forms to new uses as vehicles for the investigation and communication of truths about ordinary life; and they create in the process a tension between form and content. It is here that the inner drama of their poetry lies, and in this as in so many other important respects they represent the continuation of the essentially English tradition of equipoise in modern poetry.

2 William Wordsworth: Rational Sympathy

Wordsworth announces in his Preface to the 1802 edition of *Lyrical Ballads* that his poetry is about 'the fluxes and refluxes of the mind when agitated by the great and simple affections of our nature',[1] by which he means the fundamentally ambiguous nature of all profound human experience. His poetry is the record of his investigation into the mind's simultaneous allegiance to the realities of daily life and to the ardent pursuit of the transcendence of ordinary experience. His main task, as he recognised quite early, was to establish a poetic technique capable of communicating this to his reader. And it is important to be clear what kind of reader Wordsworth had in mind; not the single 'Intelligent Man' who is the audience of the artist, in T. S. Eliot's phrase, but something much closer to Johnson's 'common reader', for Wordsworth believed that the poet was no different from the ordinary reader of poetry except in the degree of his imaginative sympathy and in his power of expression. He therefore wished to communicate his poetic truths effectively to as wide an audience as possible by means of a rational, or philosophical language.[2] But clearly, given the unique combination in Wordsworth's poetry of a close adherence to the claims of quotidian experience and to the truths of visionary inspiration, there is a tension between his desire to articulate his understanding of ordinary reality discursively in the orderly, logical development of his syntax, and at the same time to embody a more profound understanding of the mystery of the universe in symbols. Wordsworth's solution to this artistic and rhetorical problem was to develop a rhetoric which we find employed with equal assurance in an early ballad such as 'The Idiot Boy', a meditative ode such as 'Tintern Abbey' and also in his later sonnets. It consists of a rhetoric of sympathy balanced by a contrary rhetoric of irony, a process securing simultaneous identification and moral judgement, which creates a complex effect in the reader's experience of the poetry. Thus, in his poetry as in his theory, Wordsworth explores the paradox of a poetic art in which the contrary functions of emotion and thought, of spontaneous overflow and intellectual discipline, are integrated into a meaningful whole. In his poetry we find a mystical, joyful affirmation of the universe subjected simultaneously to a moral and intellectual scrutiny. The lyrical ballad, the ode and the three sonnets I propose to discuss, works of the highest imagination, not only illustrate the theory of poetry that Wordsworth formulates so carefully in the Preface, but actually embody the imaginative truth in that theory, the moral struggle to come to terms with the ambiguity of deep human experience, and to establish and communicate the discovery as the rational, undeceived basis for the expression of joy.

Fundamentally, Wordsworth's rhetoric is rooted in his rare ability to enter fully into the experience of the human figures of his poems – 'to let himself slip into an entire delusion, and even confound and identify his own feelings with theirs'.[3] And not only people, for the poet finds 'every where objects that immediately excite in him sympathies'.[4] The reader is involved in Wordsworth's compassionate universe through pity, sympathy, or simply fellow-feeling, which gives him a sense of closeness to the poet's experience and re-creates in him the 'spontaneous overflow of powerful feelings', which Wordsworth thought should re-energise his moral sense.[5] Wordsworth employs the logic of ordinary prose syntax as the vehicle for this rhetoric because the precise articulation of feeling demands 'a far more philosophical language than that which is frequently substituted for it by Poets, who think that they are conferring honour upon themselves and their art in proportion as they separate themselves from the sympathies of men'.[6]

Thought enters the complex emotional process as a qualifying factor, for, as Wordsworth makes plain, his poetry is also the result of thinking 'long and deeply'.[7] This implies a degree of intellectual detachment, of scepticism even, allowing the moral judgement full play. Fundamental to his communication of this distancing-effect is his consistent use of irony, for, as he stresses, 'upon the accuracy with which similitude in dissimilitude, and dissimilitude in similitude are perceived, depend our taste and our moral feelings'.[8] This intellectual perspective, created by the rhetoric of irony, is embodied in the structure of the imagery, which creates a sharply distinct experience of the poem from that conveyed by the rhetoric of sympathy. Thus the vitality of the poems under discussion lies in the setting-up of a dialectic between what one might term the voice of innocence, carried by the sympathetic rhetoric, and the voice of experience presented by the ironic point of view. It is the reader's response to these two states of mind that creates the interior drama of the poems. However, it is not necessary to reject one meaning in favour of the other, for they are mutually dependent and enriching. As Wordsworth makes very clear, poetry must engage the reader's intellect as well as his emotions – 'the understanding of the being to whom we address ourselves . . . must necessarily be in some degree enlightened, his taste exalted, and his affections ameliorated'.[9] The rhetorical aim of Wordsworth's poetry is to effect in his reader a condition in which identification and judgement are held in tension; a state of muted exaltation, which Wordsworth calls 'rational sympathy'.[10]

In his Preface Wordsworth effectively describes the rhetorical and moral processes at work in 'The Idiot Boy', one of his favourite poems and among the best of *Lyrical Ballads*. It offers a profound study of a range of human experience, conveyed by a highly sophisticated rhetoric, and it also fulfils Wordsworth's own treatise on poetry. In accordance with his desire for simplicity and for direct communication, as far as possible he employs colloquial language; but, although this sometimes borders on the prosaic, and its rhythms on the comic, it is also philosophical, for it conveys ideas and emotions without evident poetic artifice. Wordsworth strives, as he says in his Preface, to make the incidents of common life interesting by tracing in them the primary laws of our nature. His central concern, therefore, is the human passions, which he pointed out are best seen in the way we associate ideas in a state of excitement, and in 'The Idiot Boy' he focuses on maternal love and on the state of mind of the mother, Betty Foy, as she reacts to the possible loss of her son, because he felt that the primary natural laws are best displayed in such unsophisticated rural folk, whose response to life is direct, urgent and unreflective. In turn this directs the reader's attention to the real subject of the poem, the ultimately unreachable, visionary mind of the idiot boy himself.

Wordsworth chose the ballad form because the ballad tradition encompasses the kind of world he wished to explore in the poem. 'The Idiot Boy' is a typical ballad in the way it deals with a domestic episode, with a single, dramatic and potentially tragic situation, with an event which happens to ordinary people, and which is presented with stark simplicity. And its central theme is love. However, as in some of Wordsworth's other lyrical ballads, the material of the poem verges on the banal and the ludicrous. Against all common sense, a mother sends her idiot son on an errand at night and on horseback to fetch a doctor for her sick neighbour. Finding its rider preoccupied, the horse stops by the path to graze. Meanwhile, fearing the worst, the mother sets out to search frantically for her Johnny and discovers eventually that he is safe. The sick woman who is the cause of all this effort and anxiety has recovered in the meantime and has come to join in the search for the missing boy. So in a sense the story is a non-event. And this is Wordsworth's point. Although the ballad form is crucial to his aims, we mistake his intentions if we concentrate on the narrative incident. As Wordsworth's Preface hints, this is a psychological ballad, not about external events as such, but employing incidents as a means of exploring the inner world of the mind which the events serve to trigger off; and it is supremely lyrical because it carries a burden of intensely felt emotion.

Wordsworth's rhetorical problem is made both easier and more difficult by the fact that the rustics respond powerfully to love and loss, but nevertheless do so in a simple way. The rural world is an inarticulate world – and Johnny's world is incomprehensible – so the poem itself becomes their verbal equivalent. It is Wordsworth's attempt to render the essentially inarticulate. In 'The Idiot Boy' his rhetoric of sympathy is conveyed through his subtle use of a narrative *persona*, who is also a poet struggling with the organisation and significance of his story.[11] His narrator engages our sympathy for his characters at a straightforward level through his obvious anxiety to retain our interest, as for instance when he is describing Betty Foy's search for Johnny:

> And how she ran, and how she walked,
> And all that to herself she talked,
> Would surely be a tedious tale.
>
> (ll.214–16)

This also operates as a means of bringing us into a relationship with the narrator, and allows him to act as our guide to the world of the poem; and one of his functions is that of posing our own questions for us:

> – Why bustle thus about your door,
> What means this bustle, Betty Foy?
> Why are you in this mighty fret?
> And why on horseback have you set
> Him whom you love, your idiot boy?
>
> (ll.7–11)

His commitment to his characters and his evident alarm for Betty and her son also engages another frame of reference, for it leads him to refer to the outside social world as a source of sympathy and judgement:

> The world will say 'tis very idle,
> Bethink you of the time of night;
> There's not a mother, no not one,
> But when she hears what you have done,
> Oh! Betty she'll be in a fright.
>
> (ll.22–6)

The narrator's voice is thus the voice of innocence in the poem. Initially he wants to know what is happening and why. But, when he learns the facts, he applies to them a standard of judgement which at first seems curiously uncomprehending of the degree of love and concern that Betty has for her neighbour, Susan Gale, and of her faith (her name after all is Betty Foy) in her beloved son.

However, it is when he comes to telling the heart of the story, Johnny's activities and their significance, that the narrator feels impelled to reveal his frustration:

> Oh reader! now that I might tell
> What Johnny and his horse are doing
> What they've been doing all this time,
> Oh could I put it into rhyme,
> A most delightful tale pursuing!
>
> (ll.322–6)

Johnny's experience, he suspects, is not the kind of truth that can be accommodated in a rational narrative structure. It is a form of knowledge that the muses, the source of poetic inspiration, deny him, and he protests in comic exasperation: 'Oh gentle muses! is this kind? / Why will ye thus my suit repel?' (ll.352–3). Instead, he finds himself driven, for the sake of the story and his reader's continued sympathy, into the realm of condescending and faintly absurd speculation about the nature of Johnny's experience: 'And now, perhaps, he's hunting sheep, / A fierce and dreadful hunter he!' (ll.337–8).

The narrator feels that his story is on firmer ground when he seeks to secure our sympathy for the psychological experience of the anguished mother, which he achieves primarily through his treatment of the poem's landscape. At the beginning it is portrayed as an ordinary rural setting:

> And he must post without delay
> Across the bridge that's in the dale,
> And by the church, and o'er the down,
> To bring a doctor from the town,
> Or she will die, old Susan Gale.
>
> (ll.52–6)

But, as Betty Foy's hunt for her lost son proceeds, the landscape becomes increasingly subjective as her fears coalesce with it, so that it comes to mirror the dimensions of her suffering mind. The night landscape ceases to be simply natural and becomes instead a threatening force, as the cliffs, the pond and the waterfall image her terrors:

> Oh saints! what is become of him?
> Perhaps he's climbed into an oak,
> Where he will stay till he is dead;
> Or sadly he has been misled,
> And joined the wandering gypsey-folk.
>
> Or him that wicked pony's carried
> To the dark cave, the goblins' hall,
> Or in the castle he's pursuing,
> Among the ghosts, his own undoing;
> Or playing with the waterfall.
>
> (ll.232–41)

The degree of sympathetic psychological penetration that the narrator achieves is apparent in the way that Betty Foy experiences a strange yet realistic heightening of her senses, for she listens so hard for Johnny that 'The grass you almost hear it growing, / You hear it now if e'er you can' (ll.295–6). And at the climax of this process, which coincides with the revelation that her son is safe, 'Her limbs are all alive with joy' (1.401).

The second mind examined by Wordsworth's narrator in 'The Idiot Boy' is that of the sick neighbour, Susan Gale, for the poem illustrates not only the mind's power of love, but also its power of healing through love. Her illness turns out to have been a psychosomatic disorder, the product of the kind of neurotic anxiety that Johnny blissfully transcends. As soon as she directs her concern outwards to Betty and her son, she begins to recover. This is a process that the narrator understands. For him the apparent magic of old Susan's cure is simply one aspect of normal human psychology, and it is given in a calm, rational, ordered syntax:

Long Susan lay deep lost in thought,
And many dreadful fears beset her,
Both for her messenger and nurse;
And as her mind grew worse and worse,
Her body it grew better.

She turned, she toss'd herself in bed,
On all sides doubts and terrors met her;
Point after point did she discuss;
And while her mind was fighting thus,
Her body still grew better.

'Alas! what is become of them?
These fears can never be endured,
I'll to the wood.' – The word scarce said,
Did Susan rise up from her bed,
As if by magic cured.

(ll.422–36)

The narrator's reference to magic is entirely appropriate to the poem's ballad context, its night-time setting, and it is consonant with a night in which mystery prevails. He thus retains our allegiance to his story, gains our sympathy for one of his main characters, yet emphasises at the same time that this is a purely natural process, which testifies to the healing-power of the mind stimulated by love.

The narrator's understanding of Betty Foy's terror and old Susan's cure throws into relief precisely what he cannot grasp, the nature of the third and most important mind explored in the poem, that of the idiot boy. The narrator, who is the reader's surrogate in the poem, shows a sympathetic comprehension of human psychology. He also gradually learns something of the moral and social ties that govern the rural world, and the bonds of love and faith that link mother and child. But he is frankly baffled by the inexplicable nature of the experience that Johnny has had. The narrator is a mildly comic figure, and, although the reader never loses sympathy with him, his naïve worldliness, his fundamental innocence and his commitment to his narrative prevent him from grasping the meaning of the experience offered by the events of the night. The narrative level of the poem, then, the rhetoric of sympathy, which is the creation of the story-teller, can take us only so far into the world of the poem.

The idiot boy, Johnny, with his repeated 'burr, burr', is even less articulate than either his mother or Susan Gale. His experience simply cannot be entered into, nor recorded, nor examined by the rational discourse of the sympathetic narrative. As Wordsworth explained in a letter to John Wilson, 'I have often applied to Idiots, in my own mind, that sublime expression of scripture that *"their life is hidden with God"*.'[12] So that, while for the narrator the idiot boy is associated with the moon and moonlight, an appropriate context for the adventure of a lunatic whose deeds he speculates are comic and inconsequential, it is central to Wordsworth's purpose to suggest the boy's sublimity. The imagery associated with his experience towards the conclusion of the poem creates a contrary rhetoric of irony, which distances the reader from the obviously sane world of the story-teller, whose point of view he began by occupying. This method allows Wordsworth to preserve the mystery of the boy's idiocy, while encouraging the reader to discover that it is in truth akin to a higher, visionary reality.

Although the sympathetic, worldly narrator posits the boy's potential activities in delightful, childlike language – he might try 'To lay his hands upon a star, / And in his pocket bring it home' (ll.330–1), or hunt the moon in a brook – this discursive hypothesis in effect merely parodies our ordered, rational world, and emphasises the gulf between the innocent view of the narrator and the boy's profound experience; a state of mute exaltation. For the conclusion of the poem is intensely symbolic and visionary. The weight of the narrator's voice has been gradually undercut by the progressively deeper resonance of the imagery, stressing precisely the 'similitude in dissimilitude, and dissimilitude in similitude' that Wordsworth advocated. For the soberly sensible narrator, and for the reader therefore, the ordinary landscape with its moonlight and owls has suggested the boy's insanity and defined it further. For Betty Foy the landscape has become the measure of her own terror and love. For Susan Gale it has provided the testing environment of her psychological drama. However, for the boy himself the worlds of madness and fear created out of our own rationality simply do not exist. For him the world of nature has been inverted, and it is through imagery of inversion that Wordsworth insists on the reality of his experience:

> And thus to Betty's question, he
> Made answer, like a traveller bold,
> (His very words I give to you,)
> 'The cocks did crow to-whoo, to-whoo,
> And the sun did shine so cold.'
> – Thus answered Johnny in his glory,
> And that was all his travel's story.
>
> (ll.457–63)

The narrator's frustrated insistence on factual accuracy and his evident disappointment at such a lame ending to his tale are counterpointed by the startling power of the imagery. Johnny's 'travel's story' is about a profound but ultimately untranslatable journey of discovery, which offers a new and valid way of seeing. Wordsworth hinted as much early in the poem when the narrator describes Johnny as being in a state of joy:

> For joy he cannot hold the bridle,
> For joy his head and heels are idle,
> He's idle all for very joy.
>
> (ll.84–6)

This is close to the condition described in 'Tintern Abbey', when with 'the deep power of joy, / We see into the life of things' (ll.49–50). As in 'We are Seven', or 'Anecdote for Fathers', it is only the narrator who needs rational explanations and who feels frustrated when none are forthcoming. For Wordsworth, as for Blake, a deeper sense of joy, of freedom, of communion with the universe – of 'glory' as Wordsworth calls it – is available only to children, or to idiots. It is a vision not restricted by intelligence, and which transcends the merely human realities of fear, illness and death.

Finally, the symmetry implied in Wordsworth's balanced rhetoric of sympathy and irony coincides effectively with the form of the poem's narrative, to which the teller of the story draws our attention explicitly at its conclusion:

> The owls have hooted all night long,
> And with the owls began my song,
> And with the owls must end.
>
> (ll.444–6)

Unlike Johnny's ineffable story, his song *must* end with the owls, not simply because of his concern with his narrative, which he wants to round off neatly, but because it registers emphatically his limited mode of perception. Moreover, this careful pattern, which mirrors the way the poem is organised around three distinct minds and three very different journeys of discovery, reveals a highly conscious rhetorical art and proclaims the existence of a fundamental wholeness and order in the universe.

The nature of poetic perception also preoccupied Wordsworth in 'Tintern Abbey', his great meditative ode written on the occasion of his visit to the Wye, which had been the scene of his personal crisis five years before. This was shortly after he had returned from France in a state of nervous exhaustion and deep depression at the collapse of his hopes for personal happiness and of his political dreams. His natural inclination to reflect on the past through the agency of memory, which provides common ground with the reader, offers the starting-point for what is in effect a spiritual autobiography. Wordsworth's endeavour to explain his moral education through the ministry of nature is articulated by the ordered development of the poem's syntax, as he contrasts past and present:

> the tall rock,
> The mountain, and the deep and gloomy wood,
> Their colours and their forms, were then to me
> An appetite: a feeling and a love,
> That had no need of a remoter charm,
> By thought supplied, or any interest

>   Unborrowed from the eye. – That time is past,
>   And all its aching joys are now no more,
>   And all its dizzy raptures.

(ll.78–86)

In this passage Wordsworth engages the reader's sympathy for his loss of the state of innocence, his forfeiture of the direct, unreflective, instinctual response to the forms of nature; and for the irrevocable process of growth into the world of adult experience. However, this rhetoric of sympathy is counterpointed by another rhetoric at work in the imagery of the passage, which on closer scrutiny is revealed as emphasising a condition, not of innocence, but rather one of ignorance. The imagery evokes a world bounded by the senses – 'colours', 'forms', 'appetite', 'feeling', 'aching joys', 'dizzy raptures' – governed by the dominant, tyrannical image of the eye, which ministers to the ego and which divorces the poet from the moral capacity for intellectual reflection. By using this rhetoric of irony, Wordsworth undercuts his nostalgic reminiscence, distances himself and the reader in judgement on the naïve egoism of his youthful self, and encourages the reader to share his own ambivalent response to his early experience. It also enables him to call upon a greater degree of sympathetic involvement as he records how in the course of his moral development he has been educated out of a totally sensual immersion in reality and into a way of perceiving that includes moral and social experience; for as the result of his own suffering he has developed from an isolated state of youthful naïvety to one of wide and profound human sympathy:

>   For I have learned
>   To look on nature, not as in the hour
>   Of thoughtless youth, but hearing oftentimes
>   The still, sad music of humanity . . . .

(ll.89–92)

An important result of that process is Wordsworth's overwhelming conviction of the essential moral value of human solidarity. This is expressed, for instance, in his Preface of 1802, in the passage which discusses 'What is a Poet?': 'Among the qualities which I have enumerated as principally conducing to form a Poet, is implied nothing differing in kind from other men, but only in degree.'[13] Yet Wordsworth is unable to ignore the uniqueness of his visionary powers. He talks in the Preface of his possessing a more 'comprehensive soul' than other men, of his joy in his own volitions and passions, and he continues, significantly, to describe himself as 'delighting to contemplate similar volitions and passions as manifested in the goings-on of the Universe, and habitually impelled to create them where he does not find them'.[14] Indeed, the central function of the rhetorical process in 'Tintern Abbey' is to register the profound tension between, on the one hand, the poet's impulse towards solidarity with the reader, and, on the other, his assertion of the absolute nature of his own way of seeing: between his experience as typical and representative, and his experience as the product of a powerful and singular imagination. The rhetoric of sympathy seeks to include the reader not only in the process of the poet's moral evolution, but, potentially at least, in the act of poetic perception itself:

> -- that serene and blessed mood,
> In which the affections gently lead us on,
> Until, the breath of this corporeal frame,
> And even the motion of our human blood
> Almost suspended, we are laid asleep
> In body, and become a living soul:
> While with an eye made quiet by the power
> Of harmony, and the deep power of joy,
> We see into the life of things.
>
> (ll.42–50)

However, simultaneous with the syntactical development of this section of the poem, which emphasises by its insistence on 'us', 'our' and 'we' the inclusion of the reader in an experience common to all men in this mood of exaltation, the ironic rhetoric in the imagery – of the 'soul', the 'eye', 'harmony' and 'joy' – proclaims the uniqueness of the poet's vision; an intense, almost mystical experience which permits a profounder, unified perception of reality. There is a deliberate tension in this passage between the rational discourse, which carries the suggestion that such moments are available to everyone, and the enactment, through the intense, vital quality of the imagery, of the exclusive, mystical nature of the moments themselves. This is consonant with the poem's larger structure, which opens by being rooted in autobiographical particularity, and returns at its conclusion to the beautifully intimate and highly exclusive relationship between Wordsworth and his sister, Dorothy.

Although the overt subject of 'Tintern Abbey' is the role that nature has played in Wordsworth's psychological and moral development, its inner drama, orchestrated by its counterpointed rhetoric, is the conflict which he felt so acutely between his need to affirm his common humanity and his equally strong fidelity to his poetic experience. This produces the reader's shared, instinctual response to the mystery of the universe, when he is at his highest pitch of ordinary perception – an intimation of 'something far more deeply interfused' (1.97), which is in 'the mind of man' (1.100); yet it also offers the profundity of Wordsworth's own creative imagination, his almost mystical vision of 'the life of things'.

In the climactic section of the poem, which precedes his moving benediction to his sister, Wordsworth's rhetoric effects, not a compromise, but an accommodation between these two ways of seeing – an assertion of the contiguity of the reader's and the poet's different yet complementary perceptions of reality:

> Therefore am I still
> A lover of the meadows and the woods,
> And mountains; and of all that we behold
> From this green earth; of all the mighty world
> Of eye and ear, both what they half-create,
> And what perceive . . . .
>
> (ll.103–8)

Here the syntax and the imagery come together in composition of a philosophical statement which grows out of the poet's and the reader's shared response to the simple but majestic objects of the natural universe. Yet it culminates in a balanced phrase which describes quite distinct and separate aspects of the inward world of perception, the world of 'eye' and 'ear'; for 'half-create' stresses the authority of the transcendental power of Wordsworth's own imagination in the act of perception – co-operating creatively and achieving union with natural phenomena – while 'perceive' denotes the reader's ordinary mode of apprehension raised to its highest level. Thus Wordsworth both recognises the unique quality of the poetic imagination, which lies at the heart of 'Tintern Abbey', and also seeks to affirm the continuum of shared experience as his testimony to the basic value of human solidarity.

Perhaps one of the most unlikely poetic forms in which to find the kind of rhetoric I have been describing is the sonnet, with its tightly intricate structure. However, it governs the three major sonnets I wish to discuss, and to ignore it produces the kind of misreading which Yvor Winters perpetrates in his dismissive analysis of 'Composed upon Westminster Bridge':

> Earth has not anything to show more fair:
> Dull would he be of soul who could pass by
> A sight so touching in its majesty:
> This City now doth, like a garment, wear
> The beauty of the morning; silent, bare,
> Ships, towers, domes, theatres, and temples lie
> Open unto the fields, and to the sky;
> All bright and glittering in the smokeless air.
> Never did sun more beautifully steep
> In his first splendour, valley, rock, or hill;
> Ne'er saw I, never felt, a calm so deep!
> The river glideth at his own sweet will:
> Dear God! the very houses seem asleep;
> And all that mighty heart is lying still!

Winters comments,

> The opening line is an example of one of the worst formulae of amateur writing: 'Earth has not anything to show more fair'. The line says nothing about the scene. 'She is the most beautiful woman I have ever seen.' 'What a glorious day!' This

is the ultimate in stylistic indolence. The next three and two-thirds lines proceed in much the same way. Then to the end of the octave we have simple but excellent description. The next three lines revert to the formula of the opening, and the twelfth line states a ridiculous falsehood in the interests of romantic pomposity: the river does not glide at its own sweet will, and this is very fortunate for London; the river glides according to the law of gravitation, and a much better line could have been made of this fact. Of the last two lines, the houses are good, the two exclamations mere noise.[15]

Wordsworth, however, is working for a much more sophisticated response from his reader, and he employs his familiar rhetoric in order to elicit a complex and realistic understanding of the modes of perception implicit in the poem.

His use of the traditional sonnet form, the octave setting the situation and the sestet clarifying and resolving the poet's response to it, supports the rhetoric of sympathy. The poem's logical development, opening with a large rhetorical statement and concluding on a note of breathless wonder, carries the burden of its joyful lyricism. The transfiguring and liberating vision of the city in rare harmony with the natural world is dominant because Wordsworth overcomes his reader's critical defences by generating suspense about the poem's subject, which is held over until the fourth line, while the developing personification of the city, and the apparently straightforward appeal of 'Dull would he be of soul who could pass by' draw on the reader's common stock of ready sympathy. The city is further humanised by the metaphor 'mighty heart', which includes the sleeping houses and the citizens in its involvement with the natural universe; a relation which includes both speaker and reader, perceiver and perceived.

But Wordsworth also wants the reader to realise that the emotion excited by the poem is in excess of its subject, and, while the logical development of the poem's syntax presents a pure, limpid vision, the sonnet has another life going on in its imagery. In one of Wordsworth's letters, mentioning an objection to his ambiguous description of the city as both 'bare' and 'clothed', he suggests how the poem's moral vigour lies in the dichotomy between its syntax and its imagery: 'The contradiction is in the *words* only – bare, as not being covered with smoke or vapour; – clothed, as being attired in the beams of the morning.'[16] Nothing stands between the beauty and the observer because the syntactical meaning is qualified by the image. Essentially, this is the process of the poem's ironic rhetoric, and it is best displayed in its central metaphor, the rapturous encounter between the sun and the city, which overtly symbolises the union of the human and natural worlds. The syntax suggests that the city wears the garment of beauty like a bride on her wedding-morning. The sun approaches as a lover, and the city lies 'open' to his fierce embrace, to be 'steep[ed]' in 'splendour'. The vitality of this sexual imagery is a powerful source of the poem's surprising revelation of harmony, but the reader is also made aware that the sense of joy it generates is qualified, for the strength of the statement makes a telling contrast with the images of torpor governing the city's response, which suggest that the union is fundamentally ironic.

This central contrast between appearance and reality is supported by the dichotomy between the houses which '*seem* asleep' and the 'mighty heart' which '*is* lying still!' (emphasis added). The sonnet's conclusion logically seems to proclaim the reconciliation of civilisation and nature, but the statement of vital harmony is undermined by the imagery so that the deep calm which the speaker experiences is dangerously seductive, producing a false sense of liberation. His observation of the river's capricious joy as it 'glideth at his own sweet will' is conditioned by a vague, idealising response, which is reversed by the final, imprisoning image of the city's dead heart. As Wordsworth remarks in the 1802 Preface, in truth the city will 'reduce [the mind] to a state of almost savage torpor'.[17]

Throughout the sonnet the innocent vision is counterpointed by one of disenchanted experience as its syntactical meaning is reversed by the imagery. The declamatory force of the opening line, proclaiming one of the earth's most glorious prospects, is ironically undercut by the concluding bathetic image, 'fair', while the neutral 'sight' and the conventional 'touching' and 'majesty', abstract and emotionally bland, imply a shallow response. Moreover, when one examines the imagery employed to evoke the city's beauty, it is curiously not there; that is, not concretely there. Its glory shrivels to the tinsel light generated by such vapid images as 'beauty of the morning', 'All bright and glittering', 'first splendour' – clichés of feeling, as Yvor Winters suggests, which produce only an emotional haze. What is more, the city's 'calm' is only majestic in direct proportion to the pulsating chaos absent from the morning scene, but kept in the reader's critical eye by such essentially reductive images as 'smokeless', by the huddle of neutral buildings and by the strange stillness of the city's heart.

The idealised vision of the city, which the speaker shares with the common reader whose sensibility is not entirely atrophied, is succinctly summarised by the lines 'Dull would he be of soul who could pass by / A sight so touching in its majesty'. But their syntactical meaning, stressing a wondering submission to the experience, runs counter to the imagistic meaning, which emphasises that only the insensate would fail to be arrested by the view. Of course Wordsworth does not disparage the idealising-tendency, but he is concerned to alert the reader to the dangers of an overflow of undisciplined feeling. This perhaps has its origin in the context of the sonnet's composition. As Dorothy's journal records, she and William did in fact pass by this powerfully seductive yet incomplete vision of harmony.[18] Wordsworth could hardly have been unaware of the personal irony, and it is this ironic, detached, intellectual perspective intercalated into the poem's structure that saves it from naïve idealism and ensures instead a balanced account of experience.

The rhetorical process is reversed in the sonnet 'I watch, and long have watched, with calm regret', in which Wordsworth explores the apparently tragic dichotomy between the world of nature and the world of man:

> I watch, and long have watched, with calm regret
> Yon slowly-sinking star – immortal Sire
> (So might he seem) of all the glittering quire!
> Blue ether still surrounds him – yet – and yet;
> But now the horizon's rocky parapet
> Is reached, where, forfeiting his bright attire,

He burns – transmuted to a dusky fire –
Then pays submissively the appointed debt
To the flying moments, and is seen no more.
Angels and gods! We struggle with our fate,
While health, power, glory, from their height decline,
Depressed; and then extinguished: and our state,
In this, how different, lost Star, from thine,
That no to-morrow shall our beams restore!

Here again one finds innocence equated with ignorance and excessive emotionalism, and experience with the stubborn refusal to be deceived. Once more the poem's syntactical development presents a coherent and self-consistent set of values, which constitute its surface meaning. In the octave the reader enters the poet's dominant viewpoint; a detached contemplation of the universe, and the quietly elegaic tone in which the limpid vision of the 'slowly-sinking star' is presented, the stately movement of the verse, its descending stress and the intimately parenthetical '(So might he seem)' all conspire to draw the reader into the poet's mood of serene wonder. But the poem's sympathetic rhetoric also depends on Wordsworth's establishment of the bleak contrast between the beautiful, ordered, cosmic drama and the human muddle and insignificance, which is sharply focused in the sestet. Like the star, moving towards the barren landscape of death, man pays his debt to time; but, while the moment of the star's eclipse is also the moment of its greatest glory, man's drift towards death ends with his achievements being simply 'Depressed; and then extinguished'. The poem's conclusion poignantly underlines the futility of man's preoccupation with progress, for like the star he is a child of time.

The sonnet's strict logic demands that we read it as a pessimistic statement of the tragic hiatus between the worlds of time and eternity. But this view, conveyed by the quiet pathos of the voice of innocence, is only one aspect of Wordsworth's vision, and the world of experience, which is revealed through the imagery, embodies a profoundly optimistic set of cosmic values which man ignores. The dominant, beautiful image of the magnificent star 'transmuted to a dusky fire' carries over to govern the sestet, where it works in conjunction with the image of 'Angels and gods!', which separates the contrasted states of octave and sestet and looks forwards and backwards with deliberate ambiguity to form part of the poem's ironic rhetoric. As the images 'immortal Sire' and 'glittering quire' suggest, the star gathers to itself the majesty of angels and gods, but it is also humanised by the image 'bright attire', and in nothing is the star more godlike than in its humanity, in its submission to the laws which govern its transience and at the same time confirm its immortality. But ironically man's sense of his immortality, his equality with angels and gods, everywhere mediated through the natural world, has been betrayed by his own egotistical, linear view of time; and in striving to become a god on his own terms – to transcend the 'flying moments' – in effect he also rejects his humanity. In contrast the star, by simply obeying the laws of the universe, transcendently fulfils itself. But, more importantly, the star is part of a profoundly optimistic vision, for its glory, its patriarchal nature, its sacrificial obedience and its final resurrection embody a religious and specifically Christian pattern of experience. This is why, for Wordsworth, the star's death cannot stand apart from its resurrection, for the point at which the eternal submits to time symbolises the continually redemptive act of God. The images of the star and of angels and gods thus serve to distance the reader in judgement on man, cut off alike from the deeper values of the temporal process and from the profounder assurance of his divinity.

What finally governs the sonnet's rhetoric is the speaker's sympathetic yet ironic relation with the star. His mood of 'calm regret' allows him the necessary detachment for a dispassionate contemplation of 'our fate', and yet it permits him at the same time to address the star in intimate terms at the conclusion of the poem. For the poet the ironic distinction between the star and mankind becomes a double irony and thus a vehicle of sympathy when the hidden parallels between their destinies is discovered to be stronger than the obvious contrasts. The sonnet's concluding lines stress this central paradox: 'and our state, / In this, how different, lost Star, from thine, / That no to-morrow shall our beams restore!' Here, as throughout the poem, the meaning of the imagery contradicts the pessimistic logic of the syntax. Clearly time serves star and sun alike, and the sunshine of man's glory, although temporarily dimmed, will like the star's majesty be restored through the inexorable process of time. The laws governing God's universe are in truth contingent upon each other, so that the star's immortality is affirmed in conjunction with time, while man's life gains significance only when placed in the context of the infinite. The poem does not lead to stoic resolution, but leads to a synthesis of sympathy and judgement in its assertion of the joy that lies beyond despair. The contrary rhetorics of sympathy and irony are thus held in tension throughout the poem as a means of being profoundly true to the complexity of human experience.

This symbiotic pattern of Wordsworth's rhetoric is most complex in the sonnet 'The world is too much with us', which is both a more philosophical and more urgently personal poem:

> The world is too much with us; late and soon,
> Getting and spending, we lay waste our powers:
> Little we see in Nature that is ours;
> We have given our hearts away, a sordid boon!
> This Sea that bares her bosom to the moon;
> The winds that will be howling at all hours,
> And are up-gathered now like sleeping flowers;
> For this, for everything, we are out of tune;
> It moves us not. – Great God! I'd rather be
> A Pagan suckled in a creed outworn;
> So might I, standing on this pleasant lea,
> Have glimpses that would make me less forlorn;
> Have sight of Proteus rising from the sea;
> Or hear old Triton blow his wreathèd horn.

The reader's sympathetic assent to the poet's position is initially gained by the implied perspective of conventional nostalgia of the opening lines, and by the poet's willingness to share the common guilt rather than to preach. However, Wordsworth deplores the spiritual hollowness of our allegiance to the commercial ethic, and the sonnet's rising note of bitterness quickly includes both poet and reader in this judgement as Wordsworth describes the sterility of life governed, not by the rhythms of the natural world, but by the shallower, more urgent rhythms of 'late and soon', 'Getting and spending', an enervating process which lays 'waste our powers', and which alienates us from a mysterious, magical harmony with nature. The radical dislocation of our perceptive faculties, 'out of tune' with nature, is juxtaposed with the tranquil harmony of the sea, the moon and the winds; and the reader's sympathy is focused more personally in the sestet, where Wordsworth's abhorrence of the stultifying effects of the commercial ideology is expressed by his preference for a discredited faith. The neurotic, fragmented experience of modern life is contrasted with the wholeness of experience offered by the ancient faith, which embodies a perception of our necessary relation with the elemental world, symbolised by the gods Proteus and Triton. The deadening, pathological preoccupation with the ego is contrasted with the direct, outward-going vision of magic and joy with which the reader comes to identify, for by the end of the poem the poet's situation is seen as an emblem of his own.

The syntactical logic of this sympathetic rhetoric suggests that Wordsworth is looking back nostalgically to a primitive pantheism. However, this is a superficial reading of the sonnet, for the balancing rhetoric of irony at work in the major patterns of imagery serves to qualify such simple assumptions, asserting the intellectual perspective of detached moral judgement. This depends, as Wordsworth pointed out, on the reader's perception of both the 'similitude' and 'dissimilitude' inherent in the triple pattern of triangular love relations which cut across the sonnet's traditional organisation. Wordsworth's loss of the ideal vision of a balanced, tripartite, mystical relation between man, nature and society is more profound than simple nostalgia can affirm, for he sees man as cut off from the ground of his being; and the poignant phrase, 'We have given our hearts away', registers his sordid betrayal of the natural world, a betrayal of instinct by will.

The ideal relation between the elements of the universe, humanity's only true model, is imaged in the sonnet's second triangular relation, between the sea, the moon and the winds; an image full of mysterious paradoxes. While the sea and the moon are traditional masculine and feminine symbols, 'This Sea that bares her bosom to the moon' is also an image at once erotic and maternal. The moon is both lover and child, while the image of the up-gathered winds suggests sleeping children. This multiplicity of relations creates a complex 'family' symbol of harmony, by which Wordsworth asserts man's need to achieve a balance between the masculine, feminine and childlike aspects of experience, for the modern ethos, which fosters the aggressive exploitation of nature, is dominated by masculine will, rather than by feminine instinct or childlike innocence.

For Wordsworth, man can only discover and fulfil his total humanity and divinity in a dynamic relation with the universe, and the third triangular relation in the poem, between the ancient poets, the gods Proteus and Triton, and the sea, proclaims that historically this has been possible. Unlike the first relation, broken by our narrow, linear view of time, and the second, ideal relation that stands outside time, this third relation depends on a profound articulation of time and eternity. At an archetypal level the elements of air and water of the second image-cluster are accommodated meaningfully into this third group of images symbolising man's natural origins. Although tabooed by the modern, Christian ethic, ancient society instinctively grasped the joy of this magical relation and incorporated it into the texture of religious and cultural experience. As mythical gods, Proteus and Triton function as symbols of their society's highest ideals. Proteus, with his ability to change his form, and Triton, with the head and trunk of a man and the tail of a fish, present cogent images of an intimate, complex harmony between man and nature, each embodying aspects of the other. The joyful humanity of gods such as 'old Triton' stresses the richness of this direct vision of man's dynamic relation with the ground of his being, a relation which subsumes the generic elements of experience as the erotic image of Proteus rising from the sea is balanced by the poet's desire to be 'suckled' in the old creed.

In this sonnet Wordsworth's rhetoric is synthesised in a union of the syntactical structures and the triple patterns of image-clusters exploring the paradox that in modern society man has set himself up as a god, but in doing so has forfeited the source of his true divinity. And not only the society but the poet himself is included in this general feeling of loss. 'Great God!', which separates octave and sestet, fulfils an ironic function in this respect, because for Wordsworth man's godhead is nowhere better manifested than in the power of the mind in creation. Thus, while the sonnet's syntactical development is sympathetic to the poet, as the pattern of imagery suggests, the poem also contains some desperately ironical self-criticism. Because of his alienation from the inner truths of the natural universe, Wordsworth is denied the poet's prophetic role. Shorn of this moral vitality, he stands in ironic contrast with the wind, in Romantic poetry a traditional symbol of inspiration, and with Proteus, who also represents the gift of prophecy. He feels the loss of the prophetic vision of the ancient poets, whose creative energy, after all, Proteus symbolises, and has retained instead only the narrow egoism bred by the materialist ethic.

While the rhetoric of sympathy ensures that the reader shares the modern poet's predicament as the spokesman for his disintegrating culture, the imagistic rhetoric of irony distances him in judgement. Rhetorically Wordsworth succeeds in presenting his poetic power at a low ebb while preserving sympathy for the poetic *persona*, and vividly evokes what has been lost while suggesting the sterility of the mind that records the process. The images of the sea, the moon and the winds are concrete and vital, but when Wordsworth describes his personal situation the imagery becomes flaccid. There is the innocuous flatness and faint archaism of the Spenserian echo 'pleasant lea',[19] which serves to emphasise, like the images of Proteus and Triton (also drawn from Spenser and Milton) that the sights he longs for are themselves the creation of literary mythology, and as such are merely symbols of a more profound, direct vision that has been irretrievably forsaken. In this sonnet the tension between sympathy and judgement is finally reconciled in the poignant realisation that the poet and society have failed each other.

The poems I have been discussing are not only works of the highest imagination, but they are also the product of an extremely self-conscious art. They permit a better understanding of the sceptical, intellectual aspect of Wordsworth's mind, an attitude which includes detached moral scrutiny as well as impulsive, joyful affirmation. Wordsworth's poetry embodies the paradox of a poetic art in which the contrary functions of emotion and thought, of spontaneous overflow and intellectual discipline, combine in a penetrating exploration of reality. His rhetoric is the communication of the 'fluxes and refluxes' of the poetic mind, and the establishment in his readers of what he calls an attitude of 'rational sympathy' towards the universe; the achievement of equipoise – a hard-won, undeceived, unembittered response of intelligent joy.

3 Thomas Hardy: Moments of Vision

As the growing list of Hardy criticism testifies, his poetic achievement is at last being given the degree of attention which has for so long been accorded almost exclusively to his novels. There had been earlier pioneering work by Samuel Hynes (*The Pattern of Hardy's Poetry*, 1956) and J. Hillis Miller (*Thomas Hardy: Distance and Desire*, 1970), but it was Donald Davie's *Thomas Hardy and British Poetry* (1973) which first drew attention to Hardy's position as a major influence on modern English verse. This was soon followed by two further critical studies – Paul Zietlow's *Moments of Vision: The Poetry of Thomas Hardy* (1974), and Tom Paulin's *Thomas Hardy: The Poetry of Perception* (1975) – and, more recently, by Dennis Taylor's book *Hardy's Poetry 1860–1928* (1981). These important books marked the beginning of a revaluation of Hardy's poetic art that had been long overdue, and, in their concern with the nature of Hardy's poetic imagination and their emphasis on the qualities of compassion and hope in his poetry, Zietlow and Paulin in particular go a long way towards redressing the balance in Hardy criticism. J. Hillis Miller, for instance, regarded Hardy essentially as a passive poet trapped in a mechanistic universe; while Geoffrey Thurley in *The Ironic Harvest* (1974) marshalled an apparently strong case against Hardy. For Thurley, because the existentialist's search for meaning can result only in total self-effacement, Hardy 'annihilates ... metaphysics, mythology, transcendence, rhetoric'.[1] Thus in Thurley's view Hardy marks the degeneration of English verse from the Romantics' pursuit of transcendence and its accompanying rhetoric of the egotistical sublime, and what has been lost in Hardy and subsequent poets, he concludes, is the '*sense of meaningfulness* associated with poetic rhetoric'.[2]

Both Tom Paulin and Paul Zietlow take a somewhat more positive view. Although Paulin regards Hardy's imagination as 'imprisoned in a Humean universe of sense-data', he also recognises that Hardy is 'somewhere between a utilitarian empiricism and a romantic idealism' and that 'he would prefer [his imagination] to have a transcending freedom, though he knows this is impossible'.[3] And Paul Zietlow affirms that Hardy's idealistic impulse leads him to place his faith in human compassion.[4] However, both these views of Hardy are limiting. For these critics too Hardy's poetry fails to achieve transcendence and his optimism is restricted to fighting a rearguard action against human suffering and misery. Yet in some of Hardy's finest verse there is considerable evidence of his imagination striving for and indeed achieving a transcending freedom, a liberation of the spirit and an abundant 'sense of meaningfulness'. In these poems Hardy can be observed strenuously seeking to establish an authentic mode of being predicated on existence itself and on his own capacity to transcend it; but the paradox of his art, at least in those poems which I would argue lie close to the heart of his poetic genius, is that he achieves the finest articulation of his existential statement within the context of the Romantic tradition.

Hardy's major achievement is his attainment of a synthesis of profound disillusion with a vitality and joy that is Wordsworthian. It has often been noted that Hardy's poetry shares some essential features with Wordsworth; he writes in the tradition of Wordsworthian ruralism, displaying the same deep feeling for the rural sense of community and human solidarity, and indeed his suffering, stoical peasantry, wresting significance from their narrow lives, are direct descendants of Wordsworth's Michael. Moreover, Hardy shares Wordsworth's profound love of landscape, his conviction of the important part that places and objects play in people's lives, and his enduring commitment to ordinary experience. But the affinity between the two poets is deeper than this. The major concern of both Wordsworth and Hardy is the relation between the human imagination and the natural world. Hardy's belief that poetry should deal with '*the other side* of common emotions'[5] echoes Wordsworth's concern in his Preface to *Lyrical Ballads* with the intensity of emotional experience and with what he calls the 'fluxes and refluxes of the mind'.[6] This is what Hardy has to say about the relation between the world of fact and the poetic imagination:

> So, then, if Nature's defects must be looked in the face and transcribed, whence arises the *art* in poetry and novel-writing? which must certainly show art, or it becomes merely mechanical reporting. I think the art lies in making these defects the basis of a hitherto unperceived beauty, by irradiating them with 'the light that never was' on their surface, but is seen to be latent in them by the spiritual eye.[7]

As Tom Paulin has pointed out, this recalls Wordsworth's description of the visionary process in 'Tintern Abbey', where the mystical experience is both perceived and created:

> Therefore am I still
> A lover of the meadows and the woods,
> And mountains; and of all that we behold
> From this green earth; of all the mighty world
> Of eye and ear, both what they half-create,
> And what perceive . . . .

And Hardy amplifies his insistence on the transfiguring power of the imagination:

> The 'simply natural' is interesting no longer. . . . The exact truth as to material fact ceases to be of importance in art – it is a student's style – the style of a period when the mind is serene and unawakened to the tragical mysteries of life; when it does not bring anything to the object that coalesces with and translates the qualities that are already there, – half-hidden, it may be – and the two united are depicted as the All.[8]

What Hardy strove for, the co-operation between the dead

world of fact and the living imagination, is, indeed, what Coleridge laments the loss of in his 'Dejection' ode, when he states that if we wish to know something beyond the inanimate cold world then, 'Ah! from the soul itself must issue forth / A light, a glory, a fair luminous cloud'.

Hardy frequently refers to Wordsworth and Coleridge in his prefaces to his poetry and in his personal writings. For instance, in his 'Apology' to *Late Lyrics and Earlier* Hardy consciously echoes Wordsworth's view, expressed in his Preface to *Lyrical Ballads*, of the importance of both the religious instinct for transcendence and the rationality of scientific reality: Hardy possesses, he says,

> a forlorn hope, a mere dream, that of an alliance between religion, which must be retained unless the world is to perish, and complete rationality, which must come, unless also the world is to perish, by means of the interfusing effect of poetry – 'the breath and finer spirit of all knowledge; the impassioned expression of science', as it was defined by an English poet who was quite orthodox in his ideas.[9]

For Hardy it is the 'interfusing effect of poetry' which incorporates both the rational world of scientific materialism and the creative, religious impulse of the imagination. It is clear that the poetry and poetic theories of Wordsworth and Coleridge were of particular significance to him in the development of his own art, and especially Coleridge's concern with the transfiguring power of the imagination. But the difference between Hardy's poetic experience and that of Coleridge is as important as the parallels. Whereas in Coleridgean terms the imagination, operating under the gentle control of the will, co-operates in a reciprocal way with the active universe in order to create a living relationship between mind and objects, for Hardy the imagination works in a somewhat different way and fulfils an inevitably different function. Unlike Coleridge's and Wordsworth's, Hardy's imagination is not intuit- ive, because, quite simply, for him there was nothing 'out there' in the universe to be intuited. Moreover, in his art the function of the imagination is not, as Coleridge suggests, to bring 'the whole soul of man into activity',[10] but rather to bring it into being. Nor can it achieve the vision of some immanent ideal, but strives instead to gain some fundamental sense of meaning grasped and articulated. This is why J. Hillis Miller's suggestion that Hardy regarded the mind as little more than a puppet of the Universal Will is too large a generalisation.[11] Although in the poem 'He Wonders about Himself Hardy admits that 'Part is mine of the general Will', like Schopenhauer, his favourite philosopher, Hardy felt that there are moments when the imagination gains its freedom, 'actuated by the modicum of free will conjecturally possessed by organic life when the mighty necessitating forces – unconscious or other – that have "the balancings of the clouds", happen to be in equilibrium, which may or may not be often'.[12]

This statement goes a long way towards explaining the relative rarity of visionary poems in Hardy's large output of verse, for it is only in this state that the poet is able to create a clearer vision of the world, a state of 'pure perception' in Schopenhauer's terms. More importantly, it makes plain that the imagination is liberated in conjunction with the will, not subordinated to it as in Coleridge's theory; rather it seems to co-operate with it in such a fundamental way, in the poems I propose to discuss, that they become a single creative force – which might perhaps best be described as 'poetic will'. Hardy's moments of transcendence are therefore very different from those of Wordsworth and Coleridge. They are not 'a sense sublime / Of something far more deeply interfused', as in 'Tintern Abbey', nor an attempt to reach beyond the material world to an ideal state, as in 'Kubla Khan'. Instead they register the achievement of meaning; they assert the joy of being here and now, and Hardy constantly seeks to establish poetic structures to capture this experience. For instance, in 'The Thing Unplanned' Hardy records a moment of daring, a sudden impulsive stepping outside the normal frame of response, the narrow groove of personality, to gain a liberating, heady sense of freedom – an action in which the poetic will triumphs over the ordinary will, which is expressive of ingrained mental habits, and thus gains a momentary sublimity:

The white winter sun struck its stroke on the bridge,
    The meadow-rills rippled and gleamed
As I left the thatched post-office, just by the ridge,
And dropped in my pocket her long tender letter,
With: 'This must be snapped! it is more than it seemed;
    And now is the opportune time!'

But against what I willed worked the surging sublime
    Of the thing that I did – the thing better!

It is important to insist on the positive quality of the poems I wish to consider, because J. Hillis Miller again overstates his case when he argues the corollary of his remark about Hardy's passivity – that in Hardy 'the act of coming to self-awareness does not lead to a recognition of the intrinsic quality of the mind [but] is a revelation about the outside world, a recognition of the mute detachment of external objects'.[13] On the contrary, Hardy's visionary poems are fundamentally a record of self-discovery and a celebration of meaning and value, and this is a process in which the obstinate facts of the external world are internalised and transfigured. Indeed the intrinsic quality of the mind is the overt subject of the title poem of the *Moments of Vision* volume. Working in co-operation with the poetic will, which functions intermittently when the universe is in equilibrium, sometimes in the depths of night, or in the moments before death, the imagination, symbolised as a 'magic' mirror which is both passive and active, has the power not only to transfigure the outer world, but to throw 'our mind back on us, and our heart, / Until we start'. It penetrates the inmost recesses of consciousness 'like a dart', making us 'such a breast-bare spectacle see / Of you and me'.

This poem displays Hardy's profound sense of the relation between true selfhood and moral identity, which is also evident in his reply to the charge of pessimism so often brought against him – that it constituted only ' "questionings" in the exploration of reality' necessary as 'the first step towards the soul's betterment'.[14] His position is the opposite of, for instance, Dostoevsky's Kirilov in *The Possessed*, who cries, 'If God does not exist, everything is allowed'. Because in Hardy the poet transcends

himself towards man, the achievement of being brings not only
enormous freedom, but also great responsibility, both to himself
and to others. Like Schopenhauer, whom he often quotes as a
philosopher of hope, Hardy stresses the central importance of
loving-kindness in human relations; he affirms the fundamental
human values of love and fellowship. And, because it thus
overcomes alienation and despair, Hardy's finest poetry also
embodies a sense of profound joy.

As Donald Davie has pointed out, there is no clear line of
development in Hardy's verse.[15] His major visionary poems
occur sporadically throughout his career because the unfettered
operation of his poetic will was a rare accident, dependent on his
sense of equilibrium in the universe. This feeling permeates 'The
Darkling Thrush', for instance, a poem of the highest imaginative
order. Apparently a modern lament for the death of God and of
nature, the poem employs a universalised and visionary landscape
to record the end of place and time:

> I leant upon a coppice gate
>> When Frost was spectre-gray,
> And Winter's dregs made desolate
>> The weakening eye of day.
> The tangled bine-stems scored the sky
>> Like strings of broken lyres,
> And all mankind that haunted nigh
>> Had sought their household fires.
>
> The land's sharp features seemed to be
>> The Century's corpse outleant,
> His crypt the cloudy canopy,
>> The wind his death-lament.
> The ancient pulse of germ and birth
>> Was shrunken hard and dry,
> And every spirit upon earth
>> Seemed fervourless as I.

This awful nullity, which is developed in the image patterns of
the first two stanzas, is mirrored in the consciousness of the poet

himself. The century's outleant corpse makes a parallel with the poet who 'leant upon a coppice gate', the 'weakening eye of day' creates a metaphor for the darkened vision of the poet, while the tangled bine-stems scoring the sky 'Like strings of broken lyres' is a further image of poetic sterility. The poet stands in mute contrast to the joyous thrush, the only other inhabitant of this ghastly landscape, and to the creative impulse of the bird's 'full-hearted' song:

> At once a voice arose among
>   The bleak twigs overhead
> In a full-hearted evensong
>   Of joy illimited;
> An aged thrush, frail, gaunt, and small,
>   In blast-beruffled plume,
> Had chosen thus to fling his soul
>   Upon the growing gloom.
>
> So little cause for carolings
>   Of such ecstatic sound
> Was written on terrestrial things
>   Afar or nigh around,
> That I could think there trembled through
>   His happy good-night air
> Some blessed Hope, whereof he knew
>   And I was unaware.

Hardy's central distinction, between the poetic sterility of the man, for whom the universe is dead, and the thrush which experiences hope and joy, appears to justify Hillis Miller's criticism of Hardy as a detached and passive observer whose poetry displays a fundamental withdrawal from life. But this view does not do justice to the complexity of the poem. Here, as in several of his visionary poems, Hardy inhabits the world of the poem not only as a neutral spectator, but also as an active participant. This duality of experience is embodied in the structure of the poem, which creates a profound connection between the two inhabitants of its desolate world, the nihilistic poet and the optimistic thrush.

Of course the thrush has a richly symbolic function. On one level its instinctive song represents the natural world's anticipation of spring and regeneration. It is also a universalised symbol of humanity. But fundamentally, 'aged', 'frail, gaunt, and small', like the poet himself, the thrush functions in the poem as its governing symbol for the continued creative activity of the poetic will, which is still at work below the level of conscious thought, and which is free to operate because the temporal frame of the poem crystalises a moment of poise in the universe. Like the poet, who is both observer and agent, the thrush creates his essential self by means of an act of will; he has '*chosen* thus to fling his soul / Upon the growing gloom' (emphasis added) – a defiant action, which images his attempt to transcend the way he has been 'thrown' into the world in an existential sense. The thrush's affirmation of the sheer joy of being in the present moment, and the accompanying sense of significance, are given peculiar force by the poem's terrible context of non-being, and by the awful irony of the poetic *persona*'s inability to grasp the meaning offered. Nevertheless, its song of ecstatic optimism, an unwitting act of loving-kindness, forges a contact between itself and the poet, creating a sense of his solidarity with all living things; and, because the thrush also represents the enduring connection between the poet and his creative imagination, the poem is allowed to stand as a courageous celebration of the poetic will, and of the possibility for the survival of undeceived joy in a world of dissolution.

Hardy also turns to his own life in order to explore the way in which the achievement of a sense of personal value is contingent on the perfect interrelation of time and place. 'The Self-Unseeing' records a moment in his boyhood when he danced in the parlour to the music of his father's violin, while his mother sat by the fireside:

> Here is the ancient floor,
> Footworn and hollowed and thin,
> Here was the former door
> Where the dead feet walked in.

She sat here in her chair,
Smiling into the fire;
He who played stood there,
Bowing it higher and higher.

Childlike, I danced in a dream;
Blessings emblazoned that day;
Everything glowed with a gleam;
Yet we were looking away!

Such moments, Hardy stresses, must be seized and understood, because, as he bleakly admits, the opportunities frequently pass unrecognised. This particular moment was unusually propitious because, as Hardy demonstrates, it was a moment of perfect universal balance. Here time, which in Hardy is always the chief threat to the achievement of joy through self-definition, is disciplined, harmonised and humanised by music and dance. As the insistent repetition of the word 'here' suggests, place is of fundamental importance in this process, not only because limited space and the present moment are the only contexts we have in which to create our integrity, but because for Hardy place contains both past and present, and therefore has the almost magical power to suspend time. Place is concretely realised by the 'ancient floor', and paradoxically by the images of feet walking and dancing, which frame the poem and reinforce the dominant image of stillness – of time annihilated by place. But the potential moment of transcendence is lost because the actions of the man, the woman and the child are involuntary. Listening to the music, they enter a hypnotic state of euphoria, which is emphasised by the heavy alliterative effect of the final stanza. The woman muses, rapt, staring into the depths of the fire; the man plays his violin in isolated abstraction; while the child dances 'in a dream'. Passive and self-regarding, they are firmly linked with the 'dead feet' at the opening of the poem, with time outside of place, time the destroyer, which they have apparently controlled, but which in truth obliterates them. That the moment described so lovingly is one of escapism rather than fulfilment is evident in Hardy's indulgent description of the cosiness of the scene; the warmth of the fire, the cliché of emotion in the phrase 'glowed with a gleam', and the ironic undercurrent that runs through the too emphatic 'Blessings emblazoned that day'. Ostensibly connected by time, manifested in music and dance, they fail to realise that what connects them fundamentally is place, the 'ancient floor' on which they act, and which symbolises a deeper and more sacramental relation of human lives. Visionary moments such as this, if grasped, offer unparalleled opportunity for people to transcend themselves by unifying acts of love, but in denying what links them they only confirm their human isolation, and, as Hardy unflinchingly records, the pleasure that they have gained is won at the cost of turning their faces away from a profounder reality.

By contrast the attainment of genuine fellowship is presented dramatically in the poem 'At the Railway Station, Upway', in which once again Hardy's strange sense of special moments of equilibrium permeating human affairs is strongly in evidence:

> 'There is not much that I can do,
>   For I've no money that's quite my own!'
>   Spoke up the pitying child –
> A little boy with a violin
> At the station before the train came in, –
> 'But I can play my fiddle to you,
> And a nice one 'tis, and good in tone!'
>
>   The man in the handcuffs smiled;
> The constable looked, and he smiled, too,
>   As the fiddle began to twang;
> And the man in the handcuffs suddenly sang
>   With grimful glee:
>   'This life so free
>   Is the thing for me!'
> And the constable smiled, and said no word,
> As if unconscious of what he heard;
> And so they went on till the train came in –
> The convict, and boy with the violin.

The station is an area of stasis where time is suspended as people occupy a limbo between trains, and where different lives come together briefly and then diverge without achieving any significant connection. Here the three figures waiting on the platform – the innocent young boy, the world-weary constable and the handcuffed convict – create a universalised image of the human condition. But fundamentally Hardy is concerned to suggest the possibility for its transformation. The child's instinctive pity for the convict and the contrasting complacent indifference of the constable establish perspectives of sympathy and irony which by the poem's conclusion have been transmuted into a unifying mood of common human charity. The boy's spontaneous act of loving-kindness in playing his violin to cheer the downcast criminal creates the grounds for the convict's transcendence of both the boy's pity and the constable's indifference. His strange, apparently ironical singing about freedom is not sheer bravado, but a profound act by which he creates a sense of his own particular momentary value. Hardy employs the apt coinage 'grimful glee' to describe the singular mood in which his stern assertion of will paradoxically produces a deeply felt liberating energy. What the moment reveals is the *'other side* of common emotions', the joy that lies beyond despair, the transcendence that can be achieved only through an awareness of tragic experience. What is more, the convict discovers in the same act not only an inner freedom, but a new sense of human responsibility, for his song is also a kindly response to the boy's overwhelming need to feel that he has somehow helped the suffering man. And through the song the convict achieves solidarity not only with the boy, imaged in the music which they share, but also with the constable, imaged in their exchange of smiles, which negates the corresponding image of the cruel manacles. Subjection has been replaced by fellowship, and the poem's dominant tableau – the boy playing his violin, and the handcuffed convict singing of freedom to the constable between trains – establishes a complex and powerful symbol of the human will triumphantly wresting significance from the tragic absurdity of daily experience.

Hardy found the metaphorical associations of railways and railway journeying fruitful, and it is instructive to compare two poems, 'Midnight on the Great Western' and 'The Change', in

which he employs the metaphor of the journey as a way of
exploring the possibilities for transcendence, with differing success.
In 'Midnight on the Great Western' the moment of poise between
one day and the next offers the journeying boy, cut off from past
and future by his trance-like reverie, the opportunity to enter the
Schopenhauerian state of 'pure perception', to gain a sense of
transcending freedom:

> In the third-class seat sat the journeying boy,
>   And the roof-lamp's oily flame
> Played down on his listless form and face,
> Bewrapt past knowing to what he was going,
>   Or whence he came.
>
> In the band of his hat the journeying boy
>   Had a ticket stuck; and a string
> Around his neck bore the key of his box,
> That twinkled gleams of the lamp's sad beams
>   Like a living thing.

As the poem grows out of the realistic limitations of the drab,
depressing railway carriage, the images collectively build into a
metaphor for life, symbolised by the key tied around his neck.
Like the poet in 'Tintern Abbey', it seems as if he has been 'laid
asleep / In body, and become a living soul' so that he can 'see
into the life of things'; and the living, twinkling key, which reflects
the dull lamplight, is a symbolic correlative of this state. But there
is a gulf between the boy and the poet, which Hardy strives to
bridge by wondering about his calmness and his lack of natural
curiosity, and he is driven to ask in conclusion,

> Knows your soul a sphere, O journeying boy,
>   Our rude realms far above,
> Whence with spacious vision you mark and mete
> This region of sin that you find you in,
>   But are not of?

As the rather flaccid, enervated and vague language of this final stanza suggests, the transaction between the'listless form and face' and the 'spacious vision' has been strenuously achieved by the poet himself, just as the key to life that the boy wears only twinkles and gleams like a living thing because it is illuminated by the sad lamp. The vision does not grow out of the world of the poem, but is imposed upon it as a form of wishful thinking. It is potential rather than actual.

However, in 'The Change' the moment of vision, of transcendence, develops naturally out of the scenic detail – the sound of the approaching train, the indifference of the crowds, the murky night, the blurred light – as the man waits at the station for his lover. It is a tense scene, at once highly personal and universal. The man is filled with impatience, with hopeful love, with a strangely heightened sense of an approaching moment of extraordinary significance. Yet when it does come it is realistically undercut both by the drab, ordinary context of the bustling railway station, and by the woman's nervous apprehension and fatigue. The ambiguity of the moment, real though it is, is given by the 'blurred lamps' which light up and idealise her smiling face, but draw attention also to her ordinary humanity. And the moment is further muted by the refrain, which places this moment of vision firmly within an ironic perspective:

> In a tedious trampling crowd yet later –
>   Who shall bear the years, the years! –
> In a tedious trampling crowd yet later,
>   When silvery singings were dumb;
> In a crowd uncaring what time might fate her,
>   Mid murks of night I stood to await her,
> And the twanging of iron wheels gave out the signal
>   that she was come.
>
> She said with a travel-tired smile –
>   Who shall lift the years O! –
> She said with a travel-tired smile,
>   Half scared by scene so strange;
> She said, outworn by mile on mile,

The blurred lamps wanning her face the while,
'O Love, I am here; I am with you!' . . . Ah, that
there should have come a change!

Everything is in opposition to this moment – the dull, mechanistic environment which is oppressive to individual feelings, the impersonal, uncaring crowds who cannot share the rapture of their meeting, the journey which brings enervation of spirit, and time which brings change and death. Yet the harsh metallic wheels announce a momentous signal and her statement of simple, profound love transcends all the warring elements in the poem. Moments such as these transcend their immediate context and convey Hardy's faith in human solidarity, loving-kindness and joy as the best things we can know. The man and the woman are there through an act of will, which is validated by the poet even though in the final line he acknowledges human fallibility, and the inscrutable workings of time and destiny. Her daring, his patience, and their faith and love combine to make this a visionary moment of profound illumination and joy.

Hardy wryly defines his own sense of alienation from the modern world, with its illusory promises of purpose, action and progress, in that splendidly visionary poem 'Old Furniture'. It is a deeply personal poem in which Hardy, although aware that 'The world has no use for one to-day / Who eyes things thus – no aim pursuing!', nevertheless courageously asserts the absolute value of his own mode of vision. Indeed the poem is organised by its many images of perception – 'see', 'eye may frame', 'I see', 'who eyes things thus', 'Creeps to my sight' – as Hardy enacts a magical resurrection. Time is brilliantly encapsulated by place, and, although the past is shown to be progressively and irretrievably past, the poem bears no trace of corrupting nostalgia, because the co-operation between place and the eye of vision, which both perceives and half-creates in Wordsworth's phrase, makes the pasts of all the generations simultaneously present:

I see the hands of the generations
That owned each shiny familiar thing

In play on its knobs and indentations,
        And with its ancient fashioning
            Still dallying:

Hands behind hands, growing paler and paler,
        As in a mirror a candle-flame
    Shows images of itself, each frailer
        As it recedes, though the eye may frame
            Its shape the same.

Hardy's juxtaposition of the living candle-flame and the cold mirror which reflects it creates a factual yet visionary image for the simultaneity of the warm hands of the past generations and the shiny, dark solidity of the furniture which they caress. Although the poem's emotion is carefully controlled by Hardy's use of homely language and by the quiet, intimate tone, there is a magical effect created by the imaginative fusion of object and vision. Insensate things come alive at the moment of vision through the co-operation of delicate images of wraithlike movement – the hands 'dallying' with the furniture, the flickering reflections of the candle-flame, the 'foggy finger' moving with 'tentative touches' to set the clock right, fingers 'dancing' over the string of the old viol – and the static, inert solidity of objects such as the clock, 'this old viol' and 'that box'.

For Hardy the neutral objects of the material world are given meaning as they are stamped by people's creative existence, and he lovingly re-creates in the vision the way their identities have been captured in the almost sacramental 'relics of householdry' around which their daily lives were built. He celebrates their love of domestic warmth (the box for tinder), punctuality and order (the finger adjusting the hands of the clock) and harmony (the music of the viol) – simple acts of human assertion which were once defined by place, but which have been apparently obliterated from the surface of things by time. Yet the values that they won from their futile routine are available to the eye of vision and are given in the poem a permanent value outside time. Hardy's identification with the past generations stresses his profound feeling for the continuity of human life, which is evident in

'Heredity', or 'In Time of "the Breaking of Nations" ', but in 'Old Furniture' his resurrection of the dead is fundamentally an act of pure loving-kindness, and, while it emphasises his isolation from the past as well as from the present, it creates at the same time a deeper sense of human solidarity.

Hardy's manipulation of time so that place is allowed to symbolise both past and present also has a liberating effect. It permits human actions to be redefined and revalued. As the generations live again, Hardy gives new meaning to their lives, and they in turn bestow on him a surer sense of being. Hardy thus creates his own spiritual values in the face of the awful inexorability of time by a supreme act of poetic will. Indeed, the controlling image of this marvellously delicate poem is that of the poetic will at work:

> On this old viol, too, fingers are dancing –
>> As whilom – just over the strings by the nut,
> The tip of a bow receding, advancing
>> In airy quivers, as if it would cut
>>> The plaintive gut.

> And I see a face by that box for tinder,
>> Glowing forth in fits from the dark,
> And fading again, as the linten cinder
>> Kindles to red at the flinty spark,
>>> Or goes out stark.

The poetic will, waxing and waning like the movement of the viol bow and the glowing face, inevitably falters and 'goes out stark'. But not before there has been an achievement of knowledge, the recognition of human fellowship, the apprehension of beautiful lives, of meaning grasped, with an accompanying spiritual renewal.

Hardy's special, almost primitive, sense of place is central to his visionary poems because for him place contains all time and preserves the significance of human actions, which can be apprehended by the poet in a state of 'pure perception'. This awareness is the controlling force behind some of the poems which focus on the loss of his wife Emma. In that moving poem 'At Castle Boterel', for instance, in which Hardy records his visit to a landscape he had once rambled over with Emma, he feels that the very place exudes her presence:

> Primaeval rocks form the road's steep border,
>   And much have they faced there, first and last,
> Of the transitory in Earth's long order;
>   But what they record in colour and cast
>   Is – that we two passed.

The fact of Emma's existence transcends time because there is an eternal record of their passing in the landscape itself, and it is this that gives life to the visionary phantom who remains on the slopes long after they have both gone. Another of their favourite haunts, the waterfall in 'After a Journey', fulfils a similar function, and the revelation of Emma's continued existence gives Hardy the courage to make his simple, faithful assertion of selfhood in the magnificent final stanza:

> Ignorant of what there is flitting here to see,
>   The waked birds preen and the seals flop lazily;
> Soon you will have, Dear, to vanish from me,
>   For the stars close their shutters and the dawn whitens
>   hazily.
> Trust me, I mind not, though Life lours,
>   The bringing me here; nay, bring me here again!
>   I am just the same as when
> Our days were a joy, and our paths through flowers.

The best example of this imaginative process, however, is the third poem of this series, 'The Phantom Horsewoman', in which Hardy employs a similar technique to that which governs 'The Darkling Thrush'. He separates the poet, described from the ironic point of view of a detached observer as a man in a 'careworn craze', from his description of the operation of the poetic will itself. As in 'Old Furniture', Hardy draws attention to the uniqueness of his imaginative process by setting it apart from the modern world of scepticism and rationalism. What he presents in the first three stanzas is the conventional view of visions as simply illusions manifested to the insane in unlikely places; obsessive fantasies associated with their pasts that often root them to the spot:

> They say he sees as an instant thing
> > More clear than to-day,
> > A sweet soft scene
> > That was once in play
> > By that briny green;
> > Yes, notes alway
> > Warm, real, and keen,
> > What his back years bring –
> A phantom of his own figuring.

This description is coloured by pity for the observer, who, like the people that watch the abstracted poet, feels the vision to be purely subjective and to bear only a limited meaning and value. And this is intensified as the stark reality of Hardy's bleak universe is captured in the dominant image of the desolate shore on which the poet stands staring at the empty waves.

But the separation which Hardy makes between the *persona* of the first three stanzas and the vision created by the poetic will in the final stanzas is his means of holding in tension the horror of the empty universe, imaged by the vacant sands and the bewildering sea mist, and the achieved joy of the meaning of being there, symbolised by the moment of vision itself:

> A ghost-girl-rider. And though, toil-tried,
> > He withers daily,
> > Time touches her not,
> > But she still rides gaily
> > In his rapt thought
> > On that shagged and shaly
> > Atlantic spot,
> > And as when first eyed
> Draws rein and sings to the swing of the tide.

The final stanzas remove the duality of the observer and the poet to allow immediacy of vision, no longer 'drawn rose-bright', but hard and clear, as Hardy creates Emma in defiance of the terrible void of her absence. She is outside time and place, yet she inhabits the place and moment of his vision. Reality and vision are united in the final stanza because Hardy only achieves this moment by facing life squarely. Although Emma is beyond time, the poet himself is not, he is 'toil-tried, / He withers daily'; and similarly life and death are held in careful balance in Hardy's description of Emma as a 'ghost-girl-rider'. Hardy's vision is not offered as a metaphysical reality, as Tom Paulin suggests,[16] nor is he withdrawing from life. In 'The Phantom Horsewoman' Hardy captures starkly the horror of a desolate universe and the awful finality of death; but he also bravely affirms that life is neither absurd nor futile if by a positive act of poetic will he can resurrect Emma, if she has a living presence in his being which gives a continued meaning to his life.

In Hardy's poetry such moments are won by the mind itself, for only the mind can give meaning to reality. Hardy's moments of vision are created out of lived experience, and their fundamental commitment to life gives them a universal validity. This wholeness of life, mind and art is perhaps best seen in what is probably his greatest poem, and the final one that I wish to consider here, 'During Wind and Rain', in which Hardy draws once more on his memories of Emma, this time of her family home in Devon:[17]

> They sing their dearest songs –
> He, she, all of them – yea,
> Treble and tenor and bass,
>   And one to play;
> With the candles mooning each face. . . .
>   Ah, no; the years O!
> How the sick leaves reel down in throngs!
>
> They clear the creeping moss –
> Elders and juniors – aye,
> Making the pathways neat

And the garden gay;
And they build a shady seat. . . .
 Ah, no; the years, the years;
See, the white storm-birds wing across!

They are blithely breakfasting all –
Men and maidens – yea,
Under the summer tree,
 With a glimpse of the bay,
While pet fowl come to the knee. . . .
 Ah, no; the years O!
And the rotten rose is ript from the wall.

They change to a high new house,
He, she, all of them – aye,
Clocks and carpets and chairs
 On the lawn all day,
And brightest things that are theirs. . . .
 Ah, no; the years, the years;
Down their carved names the rain-drop ploughs.

In some respects this is a puzzling poem and critics have responded to it in various ways. Basically the poem is divided into four discrete, beautiful moments of vision which embrace human fellowship and harmony as positive joys, each of which, however, is undercut by a remorseless refrain, which reminds the reader of the inevitable passing of time, and of mortality. A straightforward approach to the poem's meaning is to regard this division as marking a simple structural irony of the kind which operates in *Satires of Circumstance*. The vision of domestic harmony on a winter evening in the first stanza, with its magical co-operation between fact and imagination, is contrasted with the falling leaves. In the second stanza the family's instinct to combat the burgeoning of the natural world in the spring, by clearing the moss in order to make way for human concerns, is contrasted with the threatening spring gales and the malevolent storm birds. The domestication of nature is significant in the third stanza as the context for human fellowship, imaged by the sacramental breakfast under the summer tree; it too, however, finds its destroyer in time, which rips the 'rotten rose' from the wall. In the final stanza the family's removal to a new house, symbolising their courageous attempt to redefine their humanity in different places, puts their achievement of a poised, assured selfhood in jeopardy, like their furniture on the lawn exposed to the weather. Time, present in the rhythm of the seasons, co-operates with place and with human lives, yet it also carries a threat, a reminder of the inherent futility of even their noblest actions.

One view of the poem is that Hardy simply offers two distinct perspectives and allows them to stand in silent commentary on each other. Another interpretation regards these moments of vision, incomplete as they are, as having greater vividness, more impact and significance than the negative images of the refrains. But a clue to a more fruitful approach to the meaning of 'During Wind and Rain' is given by its title, which is an echo of Feste's song that concludes *Twelfth Night*, a song which is itself both a profound recognition of the fundamental absurdity of the universe and a beautiful celebration of human life and values. Hardy's poem achieves a similar transcendence. In 'During Wind and Rain' the moments of vision are not created in opposition to, or even in ignorance of, the waste and futility of life; nor are those poles of human experience permitted to stand in mute dichotomy; rather the terror of a meaningless universe is incorporated into the poem, not simply as a structural unity, but into each discrete moment of vision, subtly qualifying it and becoming part of its statement. This becomes evident if one pays close attention to Hardy's superb technique. His breaking-up of the elaborate symmetry of the four stanzas by his metrical variations in the last line of each suggests how, for the neutral observer, each idyllic moment is dissolved by a harsher reality. Yet the cluster of images conveying the delicate world of the poem also contains within it this ineluctable force of dissolution. The beautiful image in the opening stanza of the candles 'mooning each face', both factual and visionary, includes within it the suggestion of decay, for even as they illumine the gathering the candles are burning out, and the moon itself is a powerful traditional symbol of change. Similarly, the springtime vision of the second stanza comprehends the creeping moss, which remains an enduring threat to human significance; while in the third stanza the sea, which can be glimpsed by the breakfasting group, is also a potent symbol of the mutability of life and experience. And, finally, the furniture left in the open air on the lawn makes a poignant image of human vulnerability and frailty. The moments of vision themselves thus include a strong sense of an indifferent universe, of dissolution as inevitable and of human action as ultimately absurd. But this knowledge, which permeates the places in which they choose to act, is shared by the inhabitants of the world of the poem. The careful symmetry of these stanzas is the formal correlative of the way in which they nevertheless impose order and beauty on the flux of experience. Their awareness of a terrifying nullity at the heart of things is transcended by actions which celebrate love, fellowship and the sheer joy of being, which display a powerful sense of achieved selfhood, of purpose, adventure and gaiety.

To some extent the uncertainty which is still prevalent about the value of Hardy's poetry derives from the tendency of critics to regard his work as exemplifying his 'philosophy'. But, like Wordsworth and Coleridge, Hardy developed a significant part of his thinking from mature reflection upon his poetic experience. Indeed, this informs both the prefaces to his poetry and his personal writings. A more fruitful method of approaching his work than that of simply applying his ideas to his poetry, therefore, is to consider how his poetic art illuminates his thought. From this point of view, Hardy's well-known discussion of the relation between the Universal Will and the individual will, which is often regarded as the linch-pin of his thinking, is not simply an abstract formulation of his view of a deterministic universe, but is also the result of a subjective analysis of his own poetic experience. Read in the context of those poems I have been considering, Hardy's assertion of the possibility of the liberation of the will, and his insistence on the transfiguring power of the imagination explain how some of his finest poems came to be written. These moments of vision, which lie at the centre of Hardy's poetic genius, offer a positive response to modern experience, and a kind of equipoise. They rescue life from futility; they assert the significance of human values; they embody a strenuously achieved, undeceived response of profound joy, and they reaffirm in a new form the continuing Romantic ideal of transcendence.

4 John Betjeman: An Odeon Flashes Fire

As Poet Laureate, the holder of a knighthood and the most popular modern English poet, in his later years particularly John Betjeman became firmly entrenched in his critics' eyes as an establishment figure. Some attempted to relegate him to the rank of a minor comic poet – the poet of the subaltern and Miss Joan Hunter Dunn, and bicycling Oxford schoolgirls. But this view of his poetry is at best incomplete and so distinguished a poet as Philip Larkin has registered his dissent from it in uncompromising terms: 'Almost alone among living poets Betjeman is in the best sense a committed writer, whose poems spring from what he really feels about real life, and as a result he brings back to poetry a sense of dramatic urgency it had all but lost.'[1] In large measure this dramatic urgency grows out of Betjeman's intense and intimate feeling for a society caught up in profound historical change, and his poetry is a complex exploration of both the surfaces of British social life and its more secretive, inward workings. As John Press has said,

> That it is possible to convey something of the physical appearance and varied life of post-war England, the poetry of John Betjeman is sufficient proof. . . . Where Betjeman succeeds is in showing us, with such skilled precision, how his beloved Victorian and Edwardian England has been almost swept away by the new England of coffee bars, television masts, mass-produced goods, and miles of sodium-lit suburbia.[2]

Indeed, far from being a tame establishment figure, Betjeman has been a consistently subversive force in modern English verse, and in his later poetry his criticism of English society took on an increasingly angry tone. A second element in his verse, which is perhaps more prominent in his later writing, is the powerful note of spiritual anguish, and it is the urgency of Betjeman's social anger and spiritual torment which characterises his response to life as it really is. And the third important dimension of his poetry that I wish to consider is his deep commitment to communicating his perception of reality to the ordinary reader – to the rhetoric of poetry. Philip Larkin places this commitment in its historical context:

> it was Eliot who gave the modernist poetic movement its charter in the sentence, 'Poets in our civilization, as it exists at present, must be *difficult*.' And it was Betjeman who, forty years later, was to bypass the whole light industry of exegesis that had grown up round his fatal phrase, and prove, like Kipling and Housman before him, that a direct relation with the reading public could be established by anyone prepared to be moving and memorable.[3]

Although, unlike Hardy, Betjeman writes as a Christian, as Patrick Taylor-Martin has observed there is a 'clear line of descent – from Hardy and Housman through Edward Thomas and the better Georgians, to Auden and on to Larkin'.[4] Betjeman's indebtedness to Hardy is most evident in his celebration of Hardy in 'The Heart of Thomas Hardy' and in a poem such as 'Dorset', which, as Donald Davie has noted, is in imitation of Hardy's 'Friends Beyond'.[5] His early reading of Hardy introduced Betjeman to the varied uses of traditional poetic forms and strict, complex metrical structures; but more importantly his affinity with Hardy is rooted in a shared reverence for the spirit of place, for landscapes marked by the lengthy occupation of man. Indeed, W. H. Auden, who admired Betjeman's work and wrote an introduction to an American edition of his writings, coined the words 'topophil' and 'topophilia' to describe this dominant preoccupation in his poetry.[6]

In an important sense Betjeman's subversive attack on the values of contemporary English society is a corollary of his profound reverence for places. He insistently questions the validity of the concept of progress, in the headlong pursuit of which modern man heedlessly destroys both the rural community and the natural environment. In 'Dilton Marsh Halt', for instance, from *A Nip in the Air*, his defence of a small country railway station threatened with closure is not mere sentimental preservationism, or debased romanticism. The little station is worth preserving, not for economic reasons, or even to gratify the instinct of nostalgia, but because it retains for us in a vital way a closer contact with the realities of the natural world, imaged by the red sky and the cedar tree which complete the landscape – insistent reminders of our human scale, which we ignore at our peril. The poem mocks our allegiance to the illusory notion of progress, for our view of time as linear is merely the creation of human reason, expressing the human ego on a cosmic scale. Time, Betjeman reminds us, is not linear but cyclical, like the life which envelops the little station, and the poem concludes on the wryly prophetic note,

> And when all the horrible roads are finally done for,
>   And there's no more petrol left in the world to burn,
> Here to the Halt from Salisbury and from Bristol
>   Steam trains will return.

The interdependence of time and space, and the crucial importance of our retaining a fundamentally human perspective of their relation in our lives, is the subject of 'Back from Australia', from *A Nip in the Air*. The irony of the natural image in the first stanza of the 'plane travellers, 'Cocooned in Time, at this inhuman height' stresses the unnaturalness of the claustrophobic environment with its neutral-tasting food, plastic cups and the undercurrent of panic which the 'everlasting night' produces. Betjeman's savage mockery of this technological miracle and 'all the chic accoutrements of flight' is rooted in his profound awareness of how it distorts the human scale, and the second, counterpointed stanza makes a full and complete contrast as he stands with relief at home in Cornwall, looking up at the night sky. Surrounded by the permanent realities of land, sea and sky in their natural frame, he experiences a sense of space and time expanding again to their proper dimension and regaining their real significance. Seen from the human point of view, the 'hurrying autumn skies' form a dramatic and vital relation with the land as Bray Hill seems to 'hold the moon above the sea-wet sand', while the cosmic interrelation of time and space is emphatically present in the rhythm of the seasons. Betjeman's technique of contrapuntal points of view serves to stress once more the paradoxically dehumanising effect of human progress. In the totally human world of the aeroplane our attention is dominated by the paraphernalia employed to obliterate time, while in the second stanza the isolated figure standing amidst the huge grandeur of the natural world focuses our vision on the human perspective as 'the hills declare / How vast the sky is, looked at from the land', and the poet experiences the liberating sanity of true human scale.

Betjeman's concern for the preservation not merely of fine buildings but of the human frame of things which they represent, is not reactionary but, ironically in modern society with its commitment to size, growth and change for their own sakes, economically and politically subversive. As its whimsical title suggests, 'The Newest Bath Guide', again from *A Nip in the Air*, satirises 'progressive' development.[7] Old Bath with its chapels, assembly rooms, springs, terraces and sordid backstreets asserted the sheer variety of human activity. Modern Bath, however, is symbolised by the stark, monolithic structure of its new technical college. Life is now governed, not by the humanistic ethic, but by technological, commercial values, and taste now finds expression in 'working out methods of cutting down cost'. Because purely human and aesthetic needs are no longer considered significant, proportion and texture are lost in a 'uniform nothing-ness'. There is, Betjeman suggests, a fundamentally and powerfully reciprocal relation between people and their environment. The vital humanity and frank sexuality of eighteenth-century Bath have been destroyed by the Puritan work ethic, by the consequent emasculation of the city's architecture, and the climax of the poem makes a satirical statement of the concomitant profound loss of human stature:

> Now houses are 'units' and people are digits,
> And Bath has been planned into quarters for midgets.
>   Official designs are aggressively neuter,
>   The Puritan work of an eyeless computer.

Betjeman's horror of tasteless modernity emerges satirically in 'The Town Clerk's Views', from *Selected Poems* (1948), a monologue which proceeds by a carefully ascending scale of ironic exaggeration. The clerk, we discover, is a 'cool careerist', who hates variety, individualism, muddle, nature, the rural and the antique. Balanced against this is his enthusiastic approval of the modern; of concrete villas, the widespread use of glass and steel, of size, simplicity and conformity. He wants to rename Devon and Cornwall 'South-West Area One' and 'South-West Area Two', and reveals a very precise notion of what constitutes the ideal modern style. After demolishing the hamlets, he says, 'We'll rebuild the rest / To look like Welwyn mixed with Middle West.' Because in Betjeman's world there exists an intimate relation between aesthetic, moral, cultural and spiritual values, vandalism on the colossal scale proposed by the clerk constitutes a brutal assault on the whole of life:

> And ev'ry old cathedral that you enter
> By then will be an Area Culture Centre.
> Instead of nonsense about Death and Heaven
> Lectures on civic duty will be given;
> Eurhythmic classes dancing round the spire,
> And economics courses in the choir.
> So don't encourage tourists. Stay your hand
> Until we've really got the country plann'd.

Betjeman's effective use of the couplet to mirror the thumping certainty of the speaker, and the boring uniformity of his ideas, works simultaneously with the pun on the word 'views' in the poem's title, which expands as the poem develops to include a vast wasteland of visual and spiritual desecration.

The obvious political undertones of 'The Town Clerk's Views' – for it amounts to an attack on what Betjeman feels is the

totalitarian tendency of socialist extremism – are amplified more
overtly in 'Huxley Hall', from *A Few Late Chrysanthemums*. The
poet is sitting in a café in a carefully planned garden city. For
him, however, it is not the Promised Land of twentieth-century
affluence and socialist idealism, but a 'bright, hygenic hell', which
engenders a bout of deep depression and prompts thoughts about
original sin: 'In the Garden City Café with its murals on the
wall / Before a talk on "Sex and Civics" I meditated on the Fall.'
The ironic appropriateness of the modern garden city as the
context for reflection on man's banishment from the Garden of
Eden is expanded as the poem proceeds. It develops a contrapuntal
opposition between traditional Christian values and those of the
state; between the spiritual and the secular; and between the
individual and the collective. In personal terms this emerges as
a conflict between the humanistic values of the 'birch-enshrouded
homestead', symbolic of threatened middle-class individualism,
which is characterised by the 'stout free-thinker' who lives
there, and the planned, collective, predominantly working-class
environment of the new city. The contrast between the atheistical,
socialist movement that Betjeman feels is responsible for the
garden city and the passing world of religious and individual
values is seen throughout the poem in terms of the relation
between a child's world and the adult world. It is a complex
relation, which confirms in Betjeman his awareness of the reality
of original sin:

> Not the folk-museum's charting of man's Progress out of
>   slime
> Can release me from the painful seeming accident of
>   Time.
>
> Barry smashes Shirley's dolly, Shirley's eyes are crossed
>   with hate,
> Comrades plot a Comrade's downfall 'in the interests of
>   the State'..
>
> Not my vegetarian dinner, not my lime-juice minus gin,
> Quite can drown a faint conviction that we may be born
>   in Sin.

The Huxleyan world of the poem's title is both a world of dangerous innocence and one in which the inexplicable viciousness of the childhood state is also exemplified aesthetically in the city milieux. The final satiric couplet makes explicit the irony that, while the café's offering of health foods supports a materialist ethic, it ignores the health of the soul, and the perennial problem of evil.

Betjeman's criticism of bureaucracy for its blind acquiescence in the debasement of human values is developed in 'Executive', from *A Nip in the Air*, which also castigates the corruptibility of public officials by private interests. Fundamentally this poem, which records a chance meeting between a young developer and an aging preservationist, makes a savagely accurate attack on a modern idol. His role as an executive is little more than a cover for his true career, which is ironically understated as a little 'mild developing' of quiet country towns that have 'rather run to seed'. This is the source of his wealth and power. The poem's lounge-bar monologue conceals a carefully built ironic structure. At first the young man's brash assurance and obsession with status symbols seems harmless and amusing, but this mask is abruptly dropped when his urbane style and the brutal reality it habitually conceals are juxtaposed in the couplet, 'A luncheon and a drink or two, a little *savoir faire* – / I fix the Planning Officer, the Town Clerk and the Mayor.' This sudden emergence of his covert thuggery reveals him as a threat to the social order, but his type is perhaps best symbolised by Betjeman's brilliant parody of his grotesque corruption of language:

> You ask me what it is I do. Well actually, you know,
> I'm partly a liaison man and partly P. R. O.
> Essentially I integrate the current export drive
> And basically I'm viable from ten o'clock till five.

This habitual debasement of the language of ordinary human intercourse both masks and symbolises his mindless destruction of the traditional, civilised values of order, integrity and humanity; while his childlike love of dangerous toys and his boast of slaughtering pedestrians with his sports car display his fundamentally anarchic and nihilistic impulses. The fully irony of his conversation with the elderly poet, who is his silent auditor, emerges finally in the facetiously deferential tone of the poem's closing lines:

> And if some preservationist attempts to interfere
> A 'dangerous structure' notice from the Borough Engineer
> Will settle any buildings that are standing in our way –
> The modern style, sir, with respect, has really come to stay.

For Betjeman this young man is the modern hero, embodying the values of his society. And, while the new, rootless elements in English society attack its physical and moral fabric, Betjeman feels that he can no longer rely on the traditionally conservative influence of the landed classes to assert their civilising influence and prop up the tottering structure. In the savagely satirical poem 'County', from *A Nip in the Air*, he turns his anger on the county set – the 'Porkers' as he calls them. Devoid even if political principles, they have forsaken their historical sense of social obligation and surrendered to the acquisitive culture. Their world now revolves around the domestic trivia of tax-evasion, servants' wages and interminable shopping. Bereft of their social function, they employ traditional rituals to mask the hollowness of their useless lives. But the men's shooting is also a potent symbol of the anarchic, destructive instincts which threaten to pierce the well-bred vacuum, just as the social competition of the dominant women reveals neuroticism and moral fatigue:

> Bright in their county gin sets
> They tug their ropes of pearls
> And smooth their tailored twin-sets
> And drop the names of earls.

As the covert parallel in their loud talk of 'meets and marriages' implies, self-indulgent and bored, this is a predatory society, which has turned inward upon itself. Fundamentally Betjeman portrays a claustrophobic, nihilistic world, bound by meaningless tradition, but not strong enough to resist the insidious corruption of materialism. This stratum of society, affectionately dealt with in his earlier poetry, is now seen as morally as well as physically flabby. Porker is 'fat and pampered', is 'A *faux-bonhomme* and dull as well, / All pedigree and purse'. At the end of the poem Betjeman's residual sympathy for the county set comes as something of a surprise; but this is part of its covert rhetoric of irony:

> God save me from the Porkers,
>   The pathos of their lives,
> The strange example that they set
>   To new-rich farmers' wives
> Glad to accept their bounty
>   And worship from afar,
> And think of them as county –
>   County is what they are.

In Betjeman's usage 'county' has lost its traditional associations and has become a term of opprobrium; and his sympathy really implies nothing less than a damning indictment of the moribund class structure of English society, in which habitual attitudes and moral and social realities no longer reflect each other.

'Group Life: Letchworth', from *Old Lights for New Chancels*, is an even more bitter assault on the moral vacuity of upper middle-class life. It is rendered in the level of language given to the interlocutor and her respondent, who are talking about children:

> Tell me Pippididdledum,
>   Tell me how the children are.
> Working each for weal of all
>   After what you said.

This monologue ironically undercuts the values of the interlocutor, a stupidly interfering, patronising moralist who, as the respondent is fully aware, does not care about the children anyway. And the comic irony lies in the fact that the seven children – Barry, Ann, Alured, Sympathy, Wilfred, Mamie and Charlie – are not working for the 'weal of all':

> Sympathy is stencilling
>   Her decorative leatherwork,
> Wilfred's learned a folk-tune for
>   The Morris Dancers' band.

But the others are also pedalling the Kiddie Kar, taking a laxative and kicking up sand in the *kinderbank*; fulfilling themselves in various ways according to their own needs and natures. What is more, the ridiculous language –

> Wittle-tittle, wittle-tittle
>   Toodle-oodle ducky birds,
> What a lot my dicky chicky
>   Tiny tots have done.

– also registers the parent's self-congratulation, self-deception, and her reduction of the children to mere objects of possession. Moreover, the language also serves to place the speaker on the same level as the interlocutor. But, most important, the horrific quality of the parent's moral obliquity is given in the chilling interjections – made more macabre by the comic internal rhymes – 'Alured is dead' and 'I have my ex-Service man', which belong to a different moral universe from that of the children, the world of death and of cynical adult experience, but which is here made part of the children's world by the undifferentiated quality of the flow of the parent's report.

Betjeman's great gift as a social historian, his ability to record not only facts and details but mood and atmosphere, is evident in 'The Metropolitan Railway', from *A Few Late Chrysanthemums*. The poem is not really about the railway as such, although it symbolises faith in human progress, but about the people for whom it was built, and about the tyranny of time. The station buffet at Baker Street is, in Betjeman's words, a 'worn memorial' to the lives of the people celebrated in the poem. The railway itself functions as a linking and relating agent, both physically and metaphorically. It connects the city with the countryside, the realistic world of work in 'murky London wall' with the romantic advertisement world of the 'homestead set in murmuring pines', both of them milieux which govern the rhythms of ordinary life. The 'Early Electric' railway, which represents the period of suburban development, is intimately linked with the lives and loves of the people in the poem by the images employed to describe the station buffet; its 'sepia views of leafy lanes in PINNER' and the 'dazzling vacuum globes' filled with copper hearts. The railway thus functions for Betjeman as a celebration of their lives, but he also rejoices in the loving craftsmanship of the 'Bromsgrove Guild', who made the copper hearts, and in the 'radiant hope' with which 'Men formed this many-branched electrolier'.

It is a very visual poem, and it is Betjeman's imaginative immersion in the details of manufacture and the spirit of place that trigger his memories of his wife's parents. This testimony to their lives creates a kind of individual resurrection, but they also serve to personalise a raptly caught epoch of social history and they become symbolic figures, representative of all those people for whom the buffet at Baker Street station is a memorial. They also emphasise what the poet's delight in detail signals at the beginning of the poem, the feeling that places are a permanent witness to ways of living and human values. Spending the day apart in London, their daily ritual included meeting at the buffet after work and shopping, and travelling home together on the Metropolitan railway. Most importantly, however, the railway links the present with the past, connecting an era when 'Youth and Progress were in partnership' with the present reality of illness and death. This is by no means a poem of simple nostalgia; youth has turned into age, and progress has become a brutal process, as the final stanza drives home by an abrupt transition from journeys home to 'autumn-scented Middlesex' at the end of the penultimate stanza to

> Cancer has killed him. Heart is killing her.
> The trees are down. An Odeon flashes fire
> Where stood their villa by the murmuring fir

for after all they are ordinary people caught up in the real processes both of history and of life.

Betjeman's remorseless probing of the weaknesses of English

institutions includes the Church. He explores its peculiar combination of materialism and snobbery in a Browningesque dramatic
monologue, 'Bristol and Clifton', from *Old Lights for New Chancels*.
The speaker is a wealthy, urbane man, recently retired from a
position in banking, who is People's Warden of an Anglican
church, and he is addressing an acquaintance whom he has not
seen for some years. As in Browning, the almost silent auditor
draws out more of the speaker's character than he is willing to
reveal. The situation raises faint echoes of 'My Last Duchess', for
the speaker is discussing a stained-glass window, a memorial to
his wife, which he has had made for the church. The auditor is
urgently concerned with the sudden death of the speaker's wife,
of which he has just learned, but the speaker's attention is held
by the window and by himself. As the insistently repeated personal
pronoun suggests, he is a cold egoist, who makes his listener feel
acutely embarrassed:

> 'How very sad. Poor Mrs Battlecock.'
> ' "The glory that men do lives after them",
> And so I gave this window in her name.
> It's executed by a Bristol firm;
> The lady artist who designed it, made
> The figure of the lady on the left
> Something like Mrs Battlecock.'
> 'How nice.'

The fatuous quotation from Shakespeare, the unlifelike figure of
his wife tucked away to one side of the picture, and the irony of
the window perpetuating his glory rather than hers, summarises
the speaker's concern with his reputation and social position.

The reader, like the listener, is progressively involved and
embarrassed as the monologue proceeds, and the speaker warms
to his theme, for it becomes ironically apparent that this Christian
worships Mammon. His materialistic pride in the church's
paraphernalia, particularly those items, such as the new radiators,
which he has contributed, and in the collection, betrays the way
in which the church has been transformed for him into an

alternative version of his bank, as his half-joking reference to the ritualists confirms:

> Our only ritual here is with the Plate;
> I think we make it dignified enough.
> I take it up myself, and afterwards,
> Count the Collection on the vestry safe.

When the auditor enquires nervously whether their loud conversation is perhaps disturbing a woman at prayer, he receives the brusque reply that the church is due to be locked up (the bank is closing) and that in any case, the speaker says in ironic jest, she cannot be 'Loyal Church of England' if she is there simply to worship.

Appropriately the monologue ends with a catalogue of dismissive clichés and a bland assertion of his social status:

> Well, good-bye.
> Times flies. I must be going. Come again.
> There are some pleasant people living here.
> I know the Inskips very well indeed.

The speaker's suave jocularity and measured conversational tone constitute a polite veneer, which totally fails to conceal his lack of love for his late wife, the absence of any real interest in his auditor, or any care for his fellow worshippers. For him, obsessively concerned with the accumulation of tasteless property and money, the true functions of the church, embodied in prayer and ritual, are tiresomely irrelevant. The poem is a psychological study, but it expands into a criticism of the spiritually narrow, enervating, middle-class materialism of institutionalised Christianity in the modern age.

'Lenten Thoughts of a High Anglican', from *A Nip in the Air*, is a quietly whimsical poem, which on closer reading turns out to be subtly but powerfully subversive. Fundamentally it challenges not only the Church's doctrines, but the whole relevance of institutionalised religion. The poem describes

Betjeman's religious response to a beautiful woman worshipping at his church. He calls his madonna 'the Mistress' because she looks better cared for than many legal wives, and she receives from him an appropriately sexual adoration as he dwells lovingly on her eyes, lips, amused smile, expensive but nonchalant elegance and bell-toned voice. However, the poem is a carefully conceived structural irony, and his celebration of the human in a religious setting leads directly to the poem's central statement in the pivotal fourth stanza:

> How elegantly she swings along
> In the vapoury incense veil;
> The angel choir must pause in song
> When she kneels at the altar rail.

This paradox, that the divine must also worship the human, which involves a daring reversal of perspectives, counterpoints the parson's pious warning that staring around in church hinders our search for the 'Unknown God'. Like Blake in 'The Divine Image', Betjeman recognises that every man and woman is a perfectly unique centre of religious experience, and this stands in contrast to the Church's traditional teaching of Pauline theology. Betjeman suggests that we learn the world's spiritual frame by knowing its Creator in another and in oneself, and he does so with a wry yet emphatically satirical apology to institutionalised religion:

> But I hope the preacher will not think
> It unorthodox and odd
> If I add that I glimpse in 'the Mistress'
> A hint of the Unknown God.

Like Blake's child in 'A Little Boy Lost', the poet's wise innocence and imagination quietly confound bureaucratically guarded knowledge, with its emphasis on mystery, the arduous search for God, the centrality of Church ritual and the discipline of the instincts symbolised by Lent. For Betjeman the Church provides the context for worship of an instinctive and spontaneous kind.

His God frankly embraces femininity, sexuality and emancipated modernity, and there is a subdued zest in his kicking over theological and ecclesiastical traces in order to illuminate a spiritual truth.

In spite of his Christian faith, Betjeman is frequently assailed by doubt in his poetry, by a horror of death and by bouts of deep depression, and one of his best-known poems, 'Death in Leamington', from *Mount Zion*, illustrates his obsession with mortality. It is also a fine example of his subtle techniques, for, although it is deceptively lucid on the surface, this poem has disturbing depths, which are explored with considerable art, as its rhetoric gradually involves the reader in the drama.

The title contains a double irony, for the intrusion of death is cruelly inappropriate in a health resort such as Leamington, and simply incongruous in such a genteel setting, undermining our sense of human scale and values. The incongruity of death is enforced in the first stanza,

> She died in the upstairs bedroom
>   By the light of the ev'ning star
> That shone through the plate glass window
>   From over Leamington Spa

where the juxtaposition of the 'ev'ning star' and the modern 'plate glass window' brings together in the little bedroom the clashing perspectives of the eternal and the temporal. The time of the anonymous woman's death has an ironically decorous appropriateness, and its ambience is further defined by the muted echoes of Tennyson's 'Sunset and evening star' from 'Crossing the Bar'. Yet, in place of Tennyson's bold declaration of faith, Betjeman can only offer compassion for the loneliness and patience of the woman's life and death. This is registered unsentimentally by being transferred to the 'lonely crochet' which 'Lay patiently and unstirred', evoking a simultaneous sense of movement and stasis, and making a poignant link with her fingers, which 'Were dead as the spoken word'. This bleak stanza announces the end of futile activity and all human communication.

In the third stanza the focus shifts with grim realism from the dead to the living, from 'She' to the nurse. It tells us more about the dead woman's life, the routine of the sick-room and the kindly professionalism of the authoritarian figure who comes in jarringly with the tea-things amid the clutter of the 'stands and chairs'. Betjeman's main technique in this poem, his tactful shifting of emotion from the woman to the objects that composed her life, is employed at this point to make us aware that her death has been denied both a religious dimension and a dramatic context, for 'Nurse was alone with her own little soul, / And the things were alone with theirs'. Betjeman emphasises the awful, comfortless isolation of her death, while the animation of the dead 'things' intensifies our sense of the terrible inertness of the woman on the bed, and increases the dramatic irony of the nurse's ignorance.

The transference of emotion accompanies the movement of the reader's focus of interest, which is completed in the fourth stanza, for the 'She' referred to is now the nurse, and the poem's overt subject has shifted from the unfulfilled potential of the dead woman's activity to the ironic ineffectuality of the nurse's actions. These serve to deepen the reader's awareness of the reality and finality of death, for which the blinds that shut out the world are an appropriate symbol. There is also a quiet threat contained in the phrase 'She set a match to the mantel', while 'She covered the fire with coal' has its own grim symbolism.

The rising tension in the reader through his unwilling witnessing of the nurse's discovery of the woman's body reaches its climax in the fifth stanza as the sudden drama of the human voice and the futility of its impertinent injunction adds to his sense of horror: 'And "Tea!" she said in a tiny voice / "Wake up! It's nearly *five*." ' However, the sixth stanza is an arresting, chilling address to the reader, who is now involved explicitly in the world of the poem for the first time, and is forced to examine the universality of decay and death through the overt connection, urgently made, between the gradual disintegration of the material world and the inevitability of human mortality:

> Do you know that the stucco is peeling?
> Do you know that the heart will stop?

From those yellow Italianate arches
Do you hear the plaster drop?

This note of controlled hysteria intensifies the reader's suspense as the nurse's discovery of the fact of the woman's death is held over until the seventh stanza, which, like the death itself, is a release from anguish and tension. The profound silence of the calm Leamington evening which envelops the action contrasts with the sound of the nurse's voice, and the brutal fact of death is not blinked – it is there in the word 'Decaying'. However, the final stanza is the proper climax of the poem, for the reader has been led to wonder about the nature of the nurse's response to her patient's death. Yet it is also an artfully appropriate anti-climax, for it registers with tactful realism her complex human reaction, as she turns away from death and back towards life. Her professional response includes the recognition of the irrelevance of the medicine, and she moves 'the table of bottles / Away from the bed to the wall', and there is a spontaneous reverence as she tiptoes 'gently over the stairs', but she also has a sharp eye for economy as she turns down 'the gas in the hall'. Like the poet and the reader, the nurse is baffled by death, and the poem offers us no sense of its meaning. Rather Betjeman evokes in the reader the twin emotions of compassion and fear as he is implicated in the dreadful hopelessness of the quiet human tragedy, intensified by the incongruous milieu, and is forced to recognise the anti-climactic, unheroic nature of mortality.

Many of Betjeman's later poems are governed by his deepening horror at the facts of life and death; by a profound sense of doubt and loss. 'Aldershot Crematorium', from *A Nip in the Air*, is a truthful and compelling response to the modern way of death. Sandwiched between the swimming-pool and the cricket ground, the crematorium creates a dominant symbol of the casual inter-penetration of life and death, but this is only experienced fully in the shock of seeing the smoke from the furnace chimney:

And little puffs of smoke without a sound
Show what we loved dissolving in the skies,
Dear hands and feet and laughter-lighted face
And silk that hinted at the body's grace.

This brutal juxtaposition of the vital solidity of the flesh with the air into which it dissolves enforces our true reverence for the human body, particularly because our sense of another person's identity depends so much on purely physical attributes. More importantly, perhaps, the hideous incongruity of the transformation, like a grotesque conjuring-trick, denies death its proper human dimension and baffles our natural responses.

The crematorium, tastefully hidden in the suburbs, hygenic and efficient, also represents modern society's peculiar treatment of death. It is regarded as an obscenity; but, although it can be ignored, it will not go away, and the long, straight crematorium drive creates a forbidding image of its inescapable claims. This paradox is humanised as the mourners talk anxiously about the weather and the living ('Well, anyhow, it's not so cold today'), but the undercurrent of macabre irony reinforces by grim contrast their underlying thoughts of the furnace. Betjeman thus makes the whole situation of the poem focus our attention on its central paradox. Cremation emphasises so insistently the incontrovertible reality of a merely material universe that simple but profoundly human questions about a possible spiritual identity become, for the modern, sceptical age, irrelevant. Modern man seeks to escape his fear in the temporary oblivion which materialism affords; but, for a believer such as Betjeman, death presents a constant challenge to his own sense of spiritual identity: ' "*I am the Resurrection and the Life*": / Strong, deep and painful, doubt inserts the knife.'

Betjeman's anguish at being trapped in a spiritual vacuum between faith and doubt proceeds from an often appalling sense of cosmic isolation. In 'Loneliness', from *A Nip in the Air*, he explores the personal paradox of his simultaneous belief and unbelief. In tone and feeling he recalls Arnold, in 'Dover Beach' for instance, but his confrontation with his personal hell of doubt and despair is more dramatic and urgent. The poem proceeds on two levels in a vain attempt to relate the natural and the metaphysical worlds, symbolised by nature and the Easter bells; but the poem's organising-symbol is an infinitely expanding and contracting universe, which bewilders and terrifies the poet and which gives the poem its emotional tautness. The Easter bells,

with their message of assurance, open for him huge vistas of
spiritual joy: 'To deeps beyond the deepest reach / The Easter
bells enlarge the sky', but this is at once qualified by the poet's
scepticism: 'O ordered metal clatter-clang! / Is yours the song the
angels sang?', and the universe immediately shrinks to the compass
of his own timid ego:

> Belief! Belief! And unbelief . . .
> And, though you tell me I shall die,
> You say not how or when or why.

In the second, contrapuntal stanza, Betjeman seeks refuge in
nature, but there finds only further cruel paradoxes. He extends
the bitter image of himself as the last year's leaves on the beech
tree waiting to be pushed aside by new growth, for the springtime
regeneration of the natural world reminds him of the certainty
of his own decay and death. Ironically, the only possible new
growth for him will itself hasten dissolution: 'For, sure as
blackthorn bursts to snow, / Cancer in some of us will grow'.
This cruel image underlines the paradox that, although he is part
of the natural world, the poet is cut off from its cycle of death
and rebirth. Like the bells, nature is impassive to his suffering,
nor can a materialist society offer any consolation: 'Indifferent
the finches sing, / Unheeding roll the lorries past'. For the total
sceptic, the 'tasteful crematorium door' can shut out temporarily
the 'furnace roar', but for Betjeman the bells speak repeatedly of
his death, yet also hold the painful echo of what feels to him an
irretrievably lost faith. In the last stanza the sound of the Easter
bells infinitely extends a universe which is now appallingly
deserted, and which strikes answering hollow depths in his own
being: 'But church-bells open on the blast / Our loneliness, so
long and vast'. The season of natural and spiritual renewal only
deepens the irony of his terrifying isolation. The bells represent
for Betjeman what the Dover sea did for Arnold, but unlike
Arnold he can find no consolation either in human love or in the
natural world.

Although they are often located in the local and familiar,
Betjeman's personal crises often expand into a poignant statement

of the human condition. The poem 'On Leaving Wantage 1972',
from *A Nip in the Air*, explicitly records such a crisis, which is
employed to explore the complex relations between space, time,
faith and identity. Betjeman's leaving Wantage with his wife after
twenty years raises the question of the nature of human identity
in an acute form:

> I like the way these old brick garden walls
> Unevenly run down to Letcombe Brook.
> I like the mist of green about the elms
> In earliest leaf-time. More intensely green
> The duck-weed undulates; a mud-grey trout
> Hovers and darts away at my approach.

But essentially it is a poem that works through its imagery,
developing its metaphysic from the conjunction of disparate and
concretely realised images, which force the reader to adopt an
altered point of view. By the conclusion of the poem the little
brook has grown into a symbol not of place but of time, while
the church bells, which unite the vale as a physical, social and
spiritual entity, come to symbolise not Wantage but the eternal
miracle of the Christian faith which transcends time. Thus, while
the poem is apparently about a particular place and the poet's
clinging to things he loved there for reassurance of his identity –
'Friends, footpaths, hedges, house and animals' – its true subject
is time, for time is contained in place and humanised by it.
Betjeman examines the ways, both trivial and magnificent, in
which time is manifested in place. There is the tedious succession
of days, of which he is reminded by the faint reek of last night's
fish and chips, the weekly newspapers, emphasising our linear
view of time, the rhythm of the seasons and of the Christian
calendar, and beyond that stretches the whole history of Christianity and the timelessness of its faith, which is amplified into a
grand statement as the bells' 'great waves of medieval sound'

> ripple over roofs to fields and farms
> So that 'the fellowship of Christ's religion'
> Is roused to breakfast, church or sleep again.

The central paradox of the poem is that place contains all time, while here time also contains and unites place.

Betjeman's clinging to a particular place where time has been contained and ordered, where this peculiar synthesis has in a real sense sustained human identity, is an attempt to find a temporary refuge from time manifested outside place, which for the sceptic becomes an impersonal abstraction and a force of dissolution. The poet feels that time in this form is the enemy of human significance, and therefore that leaving Wantage is a symbolic act foreshadowing death, as they are whirled away, 'Till, borne along like twigs and bits of straw, / We sink below the sliding stream of time'. A further irony is concealed in the time frame of the poem, which is given as the third Sunday after Easter. Equidistant between the Resurrection and Pentecost, it reminds him of his own suspension between hope and faith, of his inability to achieve the bells' promised transcendence of time and place, and the poem ends with an honest, painful statement of confusion and loss.

Although Betjeman's poetry records a deepening horror of age, time and death, he also occasionally registers a joyful, achieved transcendence in his verse. Sometimes this is a feeling of religious affirmation; at other times it is an act of the imagination transfiguring the ordinary. In 'Harrow-on-the-Hill', from *A Few Late Chrysanthemums*, Betjeman captures the atmosphere of a melancholy London autumn evening in the trembling of the poplar trees and the threatening tapping and whispering of their grim message. But this urban world of Harrow, Wembley, Wealdstone, Kenton and Perivale, with its lighted electric trains and hissing trolleys, is transfigured by the imagination. It becomes a romantic seascape in which death can be accommodated, for now 'Harrow churchyard [is] full of sailors' graves'. The predictable, routine world of the city tea-time is transformed into a vital and dangerous universe of thundering rollers, rocky islands, gales and caves, as urban work and transport are turned into a fleet of trawlers under sail, battling to gain port.

The poem also records the process of the mind creating this movement between the worlds of reality and imagination. The first stanza proceeds by analogy. The whispering poplars remind

Betjeman of 'little breakers'. However, by the end of the second
stanza he insists on the tyranny of the imagination:

> Then Harrow-on-the-Hill's a rocky island
>   And Harrow churchyard full of sailors' graves
> And the constant click and kissing of the trolley buses
>   hissing
>   Is the level to the Wealdstone turned to waves
>   And the rumble of the railway
>   Is the thunder of the rollers
>   As they gather up for plunging
>   Into caves.

So intense is this vision that, when the poet is recalled to reality
in the final stanza, he finds it hard to realise the degree of
transfiguration that had taken place:

> Can those boats be only roof tops
>   As they stream along the skyline
> In a race for port and Padstow
>   With the gale?

Ostensibly the poem is escapist, a flight into the refuge of the
imagination. However, the imaginative process is more complex
than that, for Betjeman effects a transaction between the two
worlds, so that each includes and contains its counterpart. They
make up a unified experience because Betjeman, by his choice of
detail and his close structuring of correspondences, insists on both
modes of perception. Thus the unifying experience accommodates
both the chilling yet affectionate apprehension of the actual, and
its transcendence.

The title of 'Autumn 1964', from *High and Low*, glances back
to Keats's 'To Autumn', but the moment of vision which
Betjeman's poem celebrates is very specifically located in his
historical experience, for, unlike Keats, he lacks the secure faith
to permit his autumn to gain a fully representative, symbolic
significance. Yet the revelation which the poem records is felt to
be enough for the moment. As in Keats, Betjeman's poem develops
a series of images of natural fruition, as he delights in the sheer

perfection of the apples, the hawthorn, the creeper and the elms. The main patterns of imagery, however, are those of light and colour – 'light', 'pale haze', 'sparkling', 'bright'; and 'red', 'white', 'golden', 'yellowing' and 'green' – which together create a collective symbol of nature's abundance. Betjeman's joyful statement, 'Never have light and colour been / So prodigally thrown around', is supported by the energetic rhythm changes in the second line, giving an exhilarating feeling of intoxicating vitality.

This profound sense of nature transcending itself, emphasised in the biblical cadence of 'In half-an-hour a day of days / Will climb into its golden height', incorporates a deeply religious response, which is articulated by the affirmative ringing of the Sunday bells, the baptismal image of the sky 'washed clean and new' and the communion of the dead in the joy of the living:

> The sparkling flint, the darkling yew,
>   The red brick, less intensely red
> Than hawthorn berries bright with dew
>   Or leaves of creeper still unshed,
> The watery sky washed clean and new,
>   Are all rejoicing with the dead.

The church bells contribute to the formal unity of this carefully wrought poem, for at the end of the first stanza they offer praise, and at the conclusion of the final stanza they offer a promise of eternal love: 'And in the bells the promise tells / Of greater light where Love is found'. Through this exultant proclamation of the fundamental union between God, man, nature and the dead, Betjeman communicates a transcendent sense of the unity of all physical and metaphysical experience.

At the heart of Betjeman's poetry there lies a hard-won equilibrium of temper, and it is this fundamental sense of balance between public and private, imagination and reason, commitment and detachment, sympathy and irony, which marks the basic sanity of his poetry. This sense of equipoise controls the tone and form of 'Hearts Together', from *A Nip in the Air*, which describes an occasion in Betjeman's youth, the encounter of two adolescent lovers on a Dorset beach. Its situation and its theme – the human capacity for self-deception and the power of time to correct this distortion of values – and the colour and rhythm of the opening lines ('How emerald the chalky depths / Below the Dancing Ledge!') are Hardyesque, but the development of the poem is quintessentially Betjeman.

The lovers' sexual encounter occurs after a swim during which they pull up jelly-fishes and thoughtlessly leave them to die on a hedge in the hot sun, thus creating by an act of gratuitous cruelty their own appropriate sexual symbol:

> And lucky was the jelly-fish
>   That melted in the sun
> And poured its vitals on the turf
>   In self-effacing fun,
> Like us who in each others' arms
>   Were seed and soul in one.

As Betjeman's heavy irony stresses, they create the universe in the reflex of their own egos, and the ensuing meeting of their intellects is also incongruously and comically out of touch with reality:

> O rational the happy bathe
>   An hour before our tea,
> When you were swimming breast-stroke, all
>   Along the rocking sea
> And, in between the waves, explain'd
>   The Universe to me.

Here the familiar Betjeman counterpoint is apparent in the two distinct tones of voice which he employs – the youthful voice of innocence, carrying the rhetoric of sympathy and the mature voice of experience, enforcing the perspective of irony. These simultaneously held points of view imply perspectives of involvement and detachment, of sympathy and judgement, which create a complex effect in the reader, particularly in the final stanza:

> We gazed into the pebble beach
> And so discussed the arts,
> O logical and happy we
> Emancipated hearts.

The couple's self-consciously modern equation of rationality and happiness is simply ironic because it conceals from them the supremacy of the purely physical in their relationship, while their youthful arrogance in explaining the universe is rendered ludicrously ironic by the worlds of beauty and mystery by which they are surrounded, and which they either ignore or casually destroy. The poem's most significant irony lies in the parallel which Betjeman makes between the jelly-fish's 'self-effacing' physical death in the sun, and their own moral oblivion as they lie scorched on the beach. For Betjeman a moral universe which embraces the arts but cannot include nature reveals a profound ignorance of true human scale, and, from the point of view of the poet's maturity, an ignorance of the power of time to alter moments which seem eternally significant. So by the end of the poem the full irony of its title emerges. What he has recollected is not, as he once thought, a union of emancipated hearts, but a casual conjunction of youthful bodies and minds bound together by self-indulgence, naïvety, cruelty and egoism. True emancipation, the poem suggests, lies in the lovers' mature ability in the present to place the illusions of the past in their proper temporal frame. However, the severity of this judgement is tempered by the affectionate, mocking tone, which conveys the poet's sympathy for his own youthful self, and his realisation that his past is after all only part of a universal experience.

In Betjeman's poetry his commitment to life as it really is is balanced by his insistence on the need to maintain a comic stance towards it. In his early poetry comedy was a form of social exploration, but in his later writing it also becomes an instrument for satire and for personal defence against the horrors of age and death. In 'The Last Laugh', from *A Nip in the Air*, his final plea is not for assurance, or even consolation, but for laughter:

I made hay while the sun shone.
My work sold.
Now, if the harvest is over
And the world cold,
Give me the bonus of laughter
As I lose hold.

Betjeman's most sympathetic and perceptive critic, Philip Larkin, discussing 'The Metropolitan Railway', with its lovingly obsessive attention to the environment of Baker Street station and to the details of craftsmanship in its buffet, puts his finger unerringly on a central quality in Betjeman's writing, and suggests at the same time his place in the tradition of modern English poetry: 'Betjeman is a true heir of Thomas Hardy, who found clouds, mists and mountains "unimportant beside the wear on a threshold, or the print of a hand": his poems are about the threshold, but it and they would be nothing without the wear.'[8] It is Betjeman's insistence on the human scale, on individual values and on the need to sustain a fundamental sense of human solidarity in social life that marks his most important concerns as a writer. But his poetry is also distinguished by its twin allegiance to the qualities of realism and poetic rhetoric. Again Larkin draws attention to Betjeman's feat, in pursuing these aims, of recalling English poetry from the circular 'loop-line', as he calls it, of Modernism: 'It is arguable that Betjeman was the writer who knocked over the "No Road Through to Real Life" signs that this new tradition had erected, and who restored direct intelligible communication to poetry.'[9] What Betjeman communicates is his urgent sense of the ordinary drama of real life, and he has always in mind a real audience.

5 Philip Larkin: Reasons for Attendance

If John Betjeman 'knocked over the "No Road Through to Real Life" signs',[1] then among the major poets of the second half of this century his immediate heir is Philip Larkin, whose fundamental concern, like Betjeman, is human life lived within contemporary British society. Although not a preservationist in the obviously public way that John Betjeman was, Larkin is equally committed to the defence of an environment which reflects the good society's respect for human scale and values, and to a balance between the urban and the rural. In 'Going, Going', for instance, from *High Windows*, he registers a sense of both bitterness and panic at the rate at which the countryside is being obliterated by high-rise blocks and motorways:

> It seems, just now,
> To be happening so very fast;
> Despite all the land left free
> For the first time I feel somehow
> That it isn't going to last,
>
> That before I snuff it, the whole
> Boiling will be bricked in
> Except for the tourist parts –
> First slum of Europe . . . .

Just as for Wordsworth, Hardy and Betjeman, for Larkin too places where our lives are lived matter intensely, and on a larger scale he views our human environment as measuring society's level of culture and its quality of daily experience.

However, there is another important sense in which Larkin is the heir to a tradition running through Wordsworth and continued pre-eminently in Hardy and Betjeman. Larkin has spoken publicly of his belief in the 'fundamental nexus between poet and audience, which is something he has to struggle for in the same way that he struggles with his medium of words; indeed, it is from these two simultaneous struggles – that are in reality two halves of the same struggle – that the work of art is born'.[2] Like his predecessors in this tradition, Larkin is consciously committed to poetic rhetoric, seeing no division between poetic form and direct, urgent communication.

Almost every critic who considers Larkin's poetry finds himself, when discussing a good number of his poems, referring not to Larkin, or to the 'poet', but to the 'speaker', the 'narrative voice', or the *persona*. This is understandable with poems such as 'Wedding-Wind', 'Livings', or 'Sympathy in White Major', in which the speakers are a young woman, a businessman, a lighthouse-keeper, a don and a retired military man; but it is curious when the poems are plainly rooted in autobiography – as are 'Dockery and Son', which recalls Larkin's Oxford days, and 'The Whitsun Weddings', which records a familiar train journey from Hull, where Larkin lives, to London. What is more, even in poems, such as 'Church Going', which employ a *persona*, we frequently have the feeling that the voice in the poem is in some sense authentic – that it is the poet's own. The fact that some of Larkin's voices are close to his own historical identity and experience, while others are clearly fictional, has important implications for his relationship with his readers, for he has an unaffected desire to reach the widest possible audience. But equally important is the way that Larkin's voices are often associated with the presence of embarrassment. This is usually located in a speaker who is faced with a particular choice, or with the unfortunate consequences of past choices, and he is frequently defined as a particular kind of chooser – perplexed, or hesitant, bewildered or naïve – someone with whom the reader may find it easy to identify.[3] And of course there are those speakers who advance views of life very different from those generally regarded as Larkin's normal areas of experience; which invites the question whether he is perhaps using them to avoid the inhibiting, embarrassing presence of his own 'historical' identity as poet–librarian, as Philip Larkin of Hull. It is clear from what he has said that Larkin's reaction against Modernism grew out of what he discerned as the need for poets to create a new relationship with the reading public, and I am concerned here to argue that the essential bridge between the poet and the reader in Larkin's verse is created by means of his employment of *personae*, or narrative voices, and through the shared emotional medium of embarrassment. If this is so then embarrassment also has an important moral function in Larkin's poetry. Looked at from this point of view, Larkin is to be seen not as a wholly negative poet, but as a realist with a profound commitment to ordinary experience, yet surprisingly open to the possibility of moments of transcendence and joy.

Larkin has always felt deeply embarrassed and even indignant about the gulf that exists between his literary and social status as a poet and university librarian and that of his preferred readers, the general public. And he charges Modernism with having created this chasm. His concern for the reader in his poetry is an implicit rebuke to T. S. Eliot's notion of the poet writing for the one hypothetical 'Intelligent Man'. It is instructive to juxtapose that statement with this one of Larkin's: 'I am never particularly pleased to be told that my work is being studied by some study group. But I am pleased when people who have read one of my poems write to tell me of similar experiences.'[4] This rapport with his audience, reminiscent of that of the mid-Victorian poets and novelists, is what Larkin deliberately aims to achieve. Indeed, as he has argued at length in an essay called 'The Pleasure Principle', for him the main function of poetry is to give pleasure. He feels that this seems to have been forgotten by contemporary poets and he warns against the dangers of writing for an academic audience:

In short, the modern poetic audience . . . is a *student* audience, pure and simple. At first sight this may not seem a bad thing. . . . But at bottom poetry, like all art, is inextricably bound up with giving pleasure, and if a poet loses his pleasure-seeking audience he has lost the only audience worth having, for which the dutiful mob that signs on every September is no substitute.[5]

'The argument about Larkin', as Christopher Ricks has said, 'is essentially as to whether his poems are given up to self-pity or given to a scrutiny of self-pity and in particular to an alert refusal of easy disparaging definitions of it.'[6] Larkin himself, who is usually reticent about his writing, has felt himself driven to defend it against the charge of self-pity and also – the other side of the coin – an obsession with failure:

> One thing I do feel a slight restiveness about is being typed as someone who has carved out for himself a uniquely dreary life, growing older, having to work, and not getting things he wants and so on – is this so different from everyone else? I'd like to know how all these romantic reviewers spend their time – do they kill a lot of dragons, for instance? If other people do have wonderful lives, then I'm glad for them, but I can't help feeling that my miseries are overdone a bit by the critics.[7]

Larkin clearly considers himself to be, not a poet of 'bleak wanhope' in John Press's phrase,[8] but a realist with a deep commitment to recording and communicating the flux and texture of experience: 'I write poems to preserve things I have seen/ thought/felt (if I may so indicate a composite and complex experience) both for myself and for others.'[9] He wants to offer his readers fresh insights into the nature of that experience – 'to feel yes, I've never thought of it that way, but that's how it is'.[10]

It is true that Larkin attends to the themes of transience, loneliness, the certainty of failure and death; and his poems are sometimes ironical in tone and structure, dismal and even sad. But there are also a good many other poems – some sharply, even belligerently comic, others exquisitely lyrical – which reveal a profound curiosity about the ordinary world and a deep engagement with life. And these testify to Larkin's wish to assert the resilience of human solidarity and love. Moreover, as Andrew Motion has argued, some of his poems are concerned with achieving some sense of transcendence.[11] Charles Tomlinson's claim that Larkin is too given to a 'tenderly nursed sense of defeat'[12] is therefore surely overstated. Tomlinson also fails to remember that the voices in Larkin's poems do not necessarily speak for the whole of the author's personality. Indeed, Larkin himself has said, 'what I should like to do is write *different* kinds of poems that might be by different people'.[13]

Larkin, then, is primarily concerned with the truthful, faithful mediation of ordinary experience to as wide an audience as possible, and for him, uniquely among contemporary poets, it is embarrassment that provides the tension between the poet, the reader and reality. And he employs it essentially to overcome the formidable intellectual and social barriers that normally inhibit such communication. Indeed, as he says, his poetry is 'born of the tension between what [the poet] non-verbally feels and what can be got over in common word-usage to someone who hasn't had his experience or education or travel grant'.[14] And what Larkin often feels is embarrassment.

Larkin is peculiarly sensitive to embarrassment both in life (for many years he had a bad stammer) and in art. He frequently finds his poetry itself the source of embarrassment, as he has confessed:

> I always think that the poems I write are very much more naïve – very much more emotional – almost embarrassingly so – than a lot of other people's. When I was tagged as unemotional, it used to mystify me; I used to find it quite shaming to read some of the things I'd written.[15]

He makes embarrassment about his own past the subject of such poems as 'Annus Mirabilis', from *High Windows*, in which he wryly and humorously records his envy of the new sexual mores of the 1960s and hints perhaps at his own tardy sexual initiation:

> Sexual intercourse began
> In nineteen sixty-three
> (Which was rather late for me) –
> Between the end of the *Chatterley* ban
> And the Beatles' first LP.

And in 'I Remember, I Remember', from *The Less Deceived*,
Larkin produces a parody of a Lawrentian autobiographical poem
in which he details a childhood where nothing at all remarkable
happened:

> By now I've got the whole place clearly charted.
> Our garden first: where I did not invent
> Blinding theologies of flowers and fruits,
> And wasn't spoken to by an old hat.
> . . .
>   I'll show you, come to that,
> The bracken where I never trembling sat,
>
> Determined to go through with it; where she
> Lay back, and 'all became a burning mist'.

There are several poems in which embarrassment is treated as a
subject in its own right – for instance 'Ambulances', from *The
Whitsun Weddings*, in which Larkin unflinchingly explores our
awkwardness of response to other people's illness, as the lunchtime
crowd gathers around the ambulance to watch the patient being
stowed inside:

> And sense the solving emptiness
> That lies just under all we do,
> And for a second get it whole,
> So permanent and blank and true.
> The fastened doors recede. *Poor Soul*,
> They whisper at their own distress;

In 'The Old Fools', from *High Windows*, Larkin deals with our
shame-faced disgust at the horrors of old age – 'Why aren't they
screaming?' the speaker asks.

What do they think has happened, the old fools,
To make them like this? Do they somehow suppose
It's more grown-up when your mouth hangs open and drools,
And you keep on pissing yourself, and can't remember
Who called this morning?

But the movement of the speaker's sensibility progresses beyond this defensive brutality to a response of imaginative compassion; he learns through embarrassment and finally hopes that their lives have achieved a kind of perfection – 'the million-petalled flower / Of being here' – which transcends their physical debasement.

In the well-known 'Church Going' Larkin employs the potency of sheer perplexity (as to what churches mean) as an avenue to a deeper understanding of experience; while in 'Dockery and Son' the speaker's bewilderment and embarrassment at confronting the collapsing of perspectives of past and future in his life leads to a special kind of pondering about the mystery of human motivation. And of course there are those poems, such as 'Livings', 'Wedding-Wind' and 'A Study of Reading Habits', in which Larkin leaves the safe anchorage of his own experience, employing highly individualised *personae* to explore profounder areas of feeling without the distracting embarrassment of his own historical identity; to permit the exposure of his whole personality to a more open and enriching contact with the world.

Embarrassment is a potent force in Larkin's poetry because it registers the speaker's moral sensibility operating at the point where social and moral values impinge on his view of himself, a process which in a real sense helps to define and validate his humanity. Larkin pays careful attention to the creative opportunities provided by embarrassment because, for him, to know acute embarrassment is to realise, often in a profound way, both one's own humanity and the humanity of others. In short it has to do with our moral growth. Like joy or grief, embarrassment is fundamentally a levelling emotion, and in their shared experience of embarrassment the poet and the reader stand on common ground. There is a further moral dimension involved as well, for, if the poet or his *persona* registers embarrassment, then he (or she) gives clear evidence of his (or her) moral sensibility and trustworthiness (this after all is the psychological and moral basis of such a poem as Browning's 'Fra Lippo Lippi'). Through sharing the *persona*'s embarrassment, the reader is opened to moral impressions. And the form that offers itself as the natural vehicle for such a creative use of embarrassment is the dramatic monologue. Speaking about 'Church Going', for instance, Larkin indicates an interest in a form which he finds both congenial and versatile when he says, 'I think one has to dramatise oneself a little.'[16] Of course in Browning's hands the dramatic monologue developed into a very sophisticated form, which included a first-person speaker, whose character is unwillingly revealed, a specific time and place for the action, an auditor whose influence is felt throughout the poem, the use of colloquial language to define the speaker, and an ironic discrepancy between the speaker's view of himself and the larger moral judgement implied by the poet. Larkin employs several of these strategies in order to facilitate the reader's search for values; paradoxically by creating a fiction – for the dramatic monologue enacts its values in a special way. Yet, because of its quality of feint, of distance and objectivity, Larkin is also enabled to extend what many critics have regarded as his normal range to encompass, for instance, bitterly satirical poems as well as poems of ferocious comedy, or pure lyricism.

In some of his poems Larkin creates *personae* very unlike himself in order to explore facets of his poetic personality and open it to experience, a procedure which enables him to overcome the problem of embarrassment that might otherwise inhibit him. At the same time this strategy, which he employs in 'Wedding-Wind', for instance, from *The Less Deceived*, introduces the reader to new modes of experience, for essentially the dramatic monologue is a means by which the thought of the poem is given peculiar force by being proposed from the point of view of a speaker for whom it has a special significance. 'Wedding-Wind' is a celebration of love by a young woman on the occasion of her marriage. Throughout the poem, which maintains a sustained lyrical tone, the wind symbolises the inspirational force that has taken over her life: 'The wind blew all my wedding-day, / And my wedding-night was the night of the high wind'. Of course the speaker is a fiction, as far removed as possible from the poet himself, and some critics have found this poem not quite convincing for that very reason.[17] But this is to misunderstand the poem's strategy. We are intended to experience the young woman as a character in her own right because, in addition to the physical details of the farmyard and the stormy night – which provide circumstantial evidence to support the fiction – Larkin goes to some lengths to establish in the speaker obvious characteristics that he himself does not possess. Her flat, conversational tones introduce her as an ordinary woman, who chooses for her expression of the wind bodying forth her joy the appropriately feminine image of the unity given to beads by the thread that connects them. This detail gives validity to her sense of intoxication. When the man is absent for a few moments, she feels

> Stupid in candlelight, hearing rain,
> Seeing my face in the twisted candlestick,
> Yet seeing nothing.

And in the morning, when he has gone to look at the flood, she sets down her pail and stares at the sky and the wind. Her new experience of the power of love makes her wish to involve the whole universe in her happiness as she submits to a force much greater than herself. Although the two halves of the poem divide into night and day, the spheres of love and work, all the woman's actions are underwritten by her sense of the special significance of the wind and the dawning. Her bed is now shared by 'perpetual morning' and, although he is away from her, as the agent of this eternal dawn the man is the focus of the woman's thoughts, thus providing a strong connection between them until they are brought together in the last lines.

In 'Wedding-Wind' the dramatic monologue allows Larkin the emotional freedom to explore a romantic, Lawrentian universe; one which includes a profound sense of sexual fulfilment and joy; a world which is also evoked in the rich biblical cadence of the concluding lines:

> Shall I be let to sleep
> Now this perpetual morning shares my bed?
> Can even death dry up
> These new delighted lakes, conclude
> Our kneeling as cattle by all-generous waters?

This imagery suggests the creation of a new but immutable experience. However, it is also framed as a question by the woman, who seeks some confirmation of the validity and permanence of her joy. More importantly, it is voiced in a language more appropriate to the poet. What we experience here is a divided consciousness. We feel the presence of the speaker and are drawn to her point of view, but we are aware at the same time that she is a dramatic creation and that other perspectives exist, because Larkin has quietly intercalated them into the poem from the beginning. The man has his alternative commitment to the world of work, the horses are nervous, the woman fails to register the ominous quality of her distorted face in the candlestick; and in the second stanza the wind is still a realistically threatening force – 'hunting' and 'thrashing' – while the storm has created floods. In conclusion the ultimate limitation of the woman's happiness is mentioned – death. And it is at this point that her voice merges into that of the poet. Apart from the intrinsic pleasure that this perception of dual perspectives affords the reader, more importantly it serves to place the woman in a larger context so that the significance of her thoughts is modified by our consciousness of the existence of a more arduous and painful world. Larkin does not seek to invalidate the woman's joy; rather, he insists gently and with compassion on a broader view of the truth.

More recently, in *High Windows* Larkin has exploited the liberation from his own life and voice afforded by the dramatic monologue to explore facets of a personality which contains alternative, undeveloped lives. He does so in a fascinating triptych entitled 'Livings'. In each poem a different speaker creates a composite image of his own way of living, which is allowed to comment on the others by juxtaposition. The first poem develops the *persona* of a small businessman who deals with farmers, and who is staying at a hotel. The speaker's character is the sum of his routine, and the stale round of his life is neatly captured in the newspaper he is reading, in which the trivial and the profound are yoked in a meaningless way: 'Births, deaths. For sale. Police court. Motor spares.' His equally random connection with the regular hotel guests is quietly emphasised by the way the newspaper items are echoed by the hotel guest list in the opening of the second stanza: 'Clough, / Margetts, the Captain, Dr

Watterson'. Punctuated by empty social rituals such as standing rounds at the bar, the speaker's life is lonely and purposeless, and his mood is underlined by images of vacuity, as the stale smoke, for instance, 'hangs under the light'. Even his description of the beautiful sunset is couched in flat, dull tones, which register his numbness of response to life, while a sense of tremendous loss is also evoked by the image in the final stanza of the 'big sky' which, like his life, 'Drains down the estuary like the bed / Of a gold river'.

The revelation that the date is 1929, which is held over until the very end of the poem, creates an ironic reflection on the speaker's earlier comments and tells us more about his character than his laconic speech suggests that he is willing to reveal. There is a subdued bitterness in his observation of the hotel decor: 'The pictures on / The walls are comic – hunting, the trenches, stuff / Nobody minds or notices.' The jarring juxtaposition of 'hunting' and 'the trenches', the worlds of the shires and the battlefields, and the recognition of the irrelevance of both to the post-war age, summarises the speaker's disillusion. The rituals appropriate to the world of his father, whose business he has inherited, are no longer pertinent. History has moved on and left him stranded, as he finally realises: 'It's time for change, in nineteen twenty-nine.'

In the final poem of the triptych Larkin creates a *persona* drawn from the sphere of his own experience, but given a historical distance (Clive James believes the poem is set in the seventeenth century[18]). A young college don describes the events of an evening spent dining in college when, because of the Master's absence, there is a greater than usual consumption of wine and a freer flow of conversation. However, it is an empty ritual, not unlike that of the first poem, but here marked by displays of ponderous wit and ill temper that overlie a deeper sense of futility than even the gathering at the commercial hotel. As in the first poem we are made aware of the background presence of the social community, represented by the Master, the sizar and the butler; but again there is a lack of real communion. The desperate quality of the brittle wit is stressed by the alliteration of

Oath-enforced assertions fly
On rheumy fevers, resurrection,
Regicide and rabbit pie

and this reductive effect is enhanced throughout the poem by the rhythmic tetrameters, the jingle being emphasised by the regular alternation of masculine and feminine rhymes. Employing the don's sardonic point of view, Larkin satirises the futile conversation, and the way the values of scholarship and religious faith have been alike consigned to the college studies where 'Dusty shelves hold prayers and proofs'. Here the passing of time is the concern only of the college clocks, and even death is trivialised by his negligent reference to the college cat making a kill.

As in the earlier poem, images of inside and outside are important in developing the poem's full human context and proper scale, giving at the same time a sense of warmth and security, yet an intense awareness of human littleness and frailty. The first is achieved by the speaker's description of the piling of logs on the fire; the second by his rather academic reference to the sky where 'Above, Chaldean constellations / Sparkle over crowded roofs'. We are made to feel not only the coldness and distance of the natural world, but also the speaker's refined, aesthetic response to it. It is perceived as beautiful but inhospitable, and it is employed to register his basic impulse, which is one of retreat; not merely the comic escape from the constraints imposed by the authority of the Master, which is the speaker's subject, but a more sombre and profound withdrawal from nature, from the realities of time and death, from humane studies and from the values of religion – all of which are effectively trivialised and excluded.

The central poem records the exhilaration of the lighthouse-keeper during a stormy night. It grows out of a naturalistic context and then develops by a symbolist connection of ideas, a device which allows Larkin the freedom to be unlike himself, to be liberated from the normal, familiar, circumscribed world. It permits him to experience and convey a sense of transcendence. Far from envying the attractions of the land, where ports are 'wind-shuttered' and fleets are 'pent like hounds', where there is the warmth of 'Fires in humped inns / Kippering sea-pictures' (a world which, as the imagery suggests, is secure, confined, even domesticated), the speaker feels at one with the weather and the sea. He is enveloped by an animate universe:

> The sea explodes upwards,
> Relapsing, to slaver
> Off landing-stage steps –
> . . .
> Rocks writhe back to sight.
> Mussels, limpets,
> Husband their tenacity
> In the freezing slither . . .

And there is the beautifully sensuous, transfiguring image of the whirling snow like a delicate cloud of moths around the lamp on a summer night. The speaker experiences a profound sense of joyful communion, which is emphasised by the concluding lines of the first two stanzas: 'Running suds, rejoice!', 'Creatures, I cherish you!' as he luxuriates in the power and activity of the natural world, and in its reciprocal relation with his own imagination. Indeed, the keeper's whole universe is governed by the intensity of his imagination as it feeds upon its own isolation – 'Radio rubs its legs, / Telling me of elsewhere'. As his reference to divining-cards implies, he is a man reduced to fundamentals, profoundly in touch with the primitive elements both in the outside world and within himself. Glad to be isolated in nature, he feels himself to be 'Guarded by brilliance' and he experiences an almost mystical state of calm amidst the frenzy of the storm. Initially this frame of mind seems to the reader to indicate a kind of madness, except that for the speaker, whose point of view carries overwhelming conviction by the sheer energy of his language, it is the social world that is insane as 'Lit shelved liners / Grope like mad worlds westward.'

In 'Livings' Larkin's use of *personae* frees him to explore the values associated with three ways of living, and he displays in the process an acute historical and geographical imagination, an ability to create psychologically convincing figures, and moral sympathy. By probing various social and moral values in different periods and places, he expands the reader's understanding of the sheer variety and complexity of ordinary lived experience. Moreover, by framing the central poem of exuberant energy and lyrical splendour with two that record defeat and disillusion, he is concerned to affirm the deeper values of solitude and communion with the natural world, which produce a sense of wholeness within the self, and a joyful experience of transcendence.

One of Larkin's most successful poems is 'Church Going', from *The Less Deceived*, which involves one of his most sophisticated uses of the *persona*. It employs a typical symbolist strategy for, as John Wain has pointed out, 'in terms of ancestry, the central figure is descended from late nineteenth century poetry (Laforge and Corbière), the intermediary being Mr Eliot's Prufrock'.[19] He is an awkward, embarrassed figure with whom the reader can readily identify. John Press recognises that the speaker in the poem is fictional, but he finds it impossible to believe in the character because his clumsy references to the church's 'holy end' are incompatible with his esoteric knowledge of roodlofts and pyx. Moreover, Press wonders how the awkward man figured at the opening of the poem could articulate the weighty peroration of the magnificent final stanza.[20] However, as the last stanza itself indicates, the poem is about the need to 'grow wise', and its development is fundamentally concerned with revealing a growth in wisdom achieved not by visiting one church, but through the habit of church-going itself.

The speaker at the beginning of the poem is essentially the reader's representative. As most of us have done at some time or other, he mounts the lectern only to feel baffled and embarrassed. But by the poem's conclusion the speaker has effectively attained, through reflection, the wisdom evinced by the poet. The reader thus gradually adopts a perspective larger than that of the *persona* with whom he has been identifying, and which the poet finally confirms in his own authoritative voice. This method confers on the poem a more precise and subtle inner form than its overt structure of situation, reflection and statement would suggest. The monologue exists as the vehicle for both Larkin's opinions and the development of the experience which informs those views and gives them validity, a process in which embarrassment has a significant part to play. In 'Church Going' Larkin presents the movement from a divided to a unified consciousness; that is, from our sense of a gulf between the poet and the *persona* (for whom churches are bewildering, embarrassing and meaningless) to a point at which the accumulated experience of the speaker, the reader and the poet finally coincide in the concluding coherent statement of affirmation.

Larkin dramatises shifts in the speaker's mind by variations in tone which record significant fluctuations of emotion. We learn a good deal about the fictional speaker from detail; for instance, from the embarrassed joke about the silence 'Brewed God knows how long', which accompanies the removal of his cycle clips, and his casual assessment of the contents of the church. It is a telling moment of off-guardedness, of 'awkward reverence', and the poem develops from the recognition of what this gesture means. He is clearly unsatisfied and he uses the paraphernalia of the building to explore its possible significance for him. His attempt to parody the vicar or lay reader is a gesture towards understanding, but the 'unignorable silence' makes mere speech seem vain and silly. Moreover, the 'Hectoring large-scale verses' that he reads contrast strongly with the eloquent peroration at the close of the poem, which offers less assurance, but has the compelling air of truth. The 'Here endeth' which the speaker announces to the church's sniggering echoes is ambiguous. It marks the conclusion of his futile attempts to comprehend the meaning of the place, but it also signifies the collapse of the Church and the demise of faith, which are developed in the succeeding stanzas, so that by the end of the poem the speaker's parody of Church ritual has assumed wider significance.

As he goes on to speculate on what will happen when the churches fall out of use, the speaker begins to understand something of their function in human life. At first his mood remains jocular to cover his embarrassment, as for example in the alliteration of 'parchment, plate and pyx', but the gradual change to a mood of nervous apprehension is indicated by his use of archaisms. He presents a very literal picture of the church in decay, and the other figures in the poem – the 'dubious women', the 'ruin-bibber, randy for antique', people whose simple superstitions of superficial cultural appetites will miss the significance of the place, and his future 'representative', ignorant and bored – are all used to define for himself the function and meaning of the church. Indeed, the fact that the speaker feels pressured to mock these absurd people also reveals a desire on his part to protect the sanctity of the ground.

The wisdom that the speaker gains from church-going is the knowledge that the church is the source of 'Power of some sort or other', not because of its impressive interior, for he has 'no idea / What this accoutred frowsty barn is worth', but because it symbolises the fundamental needs of the human spirit. The roots of culture lie in the immemorial rituals associated with birth, marriage and death which have been celebrated on this spot, and it is for this reason that he says, 'It pleases me to stand in silence here'. The conclusion of the poem is controlled by the poet's own voice, which the evolving understanding of the speaker permits to emerge naturally, while the contrast between the poet and his representative in the future, who will lack his opportunity to acquire wisdom, releases its final, elevated, sonorous statement of affirmation. The casual, colloquial speech patterns of the earlier speaker are gradually abandoned in favour of the rhetorical and the lyrical:

> A serious house on serious earth it is,
> In whose blent air all our compulsions meet,
> Are recognised, and robed as destinies.
> And that much never can be obsolete,
> Since someone will forever be surprising
> A hunger in himself to be more serious,
> And gravitating with it to this ground,
> Which, he once heard, was proper to grow wise in,
> If only that so many dead lie round.

Larkin's embarrassment at the gulf that exists between contemporary poetry and the general reading public is the main impulse behind 'A Study of Reading Habits', from *The Whitsun Weddings*. In this poem Larkin probes the issues implicit in the ways that reading impinges on the lives of ordinary people. As the poem's title indicates, reading is a socially acquired habit which embodies society's values. The speaker records how it ministered to his boyhood need to identify with hero figures, and how in adolescence it fed his sexual imagination, but now that he has reached middle age he has to admit that he can no longer identify with supermen, nor with the brutal sexuality of the villains of his earlier fantasies. Instead he sees himself as the unreliable dude who lets the girl down before the hero arrives, or as the cowardly store-keeper. For him, as for many people, reading simply provides an escape from reality – it 'Cured most things short of school'. Now he no longer reads much because of his painfully acquired knowledge of the real relation between fiction and life. Reading has let him down because among the stereotypes that fiction offers there are also the failures and the cowards – the ordinary man written larger than life – and this tardy but inescapable identification is simply too much to bear.

The character of the speaker is developed by playing off his colloquial language against the language of the literature that he recalls reading as a boy, when he dealt out 'the old right hook / To dirty dogs twice my size', and, as an adolescent, 'The women I clubbed with sex! / I broke them up like meringues.' Larkin captures exactly his tone of nostalgic reminiscence, his breathless sexual excitement, his laconic admission of failure, and his final explosive imprecation, 'Get stewed: / Books are a load of crap.' This is not Larkin adopting an anti-intellectual pose. Rather, our awareness that the controlling consciousness of the poem is that of a poet-librarian releases, together with the sympathy that the speaker's revelation demands, its basically comic and anarchic impulse. But it is also a serious poem, in which Larkin shows considerable insight into the kinds of claim that the ordinary reader is taught to make upon fiction, and he raises important questions (as the title implies, it is a 'study') about the nature and function of literature in our society.

In Larkin's dramatic monologues speakers such as this one are often designed to arouse our concern for the oppressed or disadvantaged, and a similar, bitter, bewildered embarrassment – this time about the way life has gone wrong – gives rise to the ferocious humour of such a poem as 'Send No Money', from *The Whitsun Weddings*, in which the *persona*, who is a young man, asks Time to tell him the way things go. However, insight into the nature of life simply comes too late for him, and in any case it is useless:

> Half life is over now,
> And I meet full face on dark mornings
> The bestial visor, bent in
> By the blows of what happened to happen.
> What does it prove? Sod all.
> In this way I spent youth,
> Tracing the trite untransferable
> Truss-advertisement, truth.

This final line brilliantly suggests both the artificial support and the false promise of youth. The speaker is embarrassed and embittered to discover that the missed opportunities of the past are what compose his present existence.

Embarrassment is an emotion very close to indignation, a way of coping with anger, and in a satiric poem such as 'Naturally the Foundation will Bear Your Expenses', from *The Whitsun Weddings*, Larkin manages both to mask his embarrassment and give vent to his moral indignation through the employment of a very different *persona*. It is a comic poem, but, as Larkin has pointed out, it is also 'as serious as anything I have written'.[21] It concerns a young English academic who is on his way to India to deliver a lecture that he has already given at Berkeley and which he intends to read on the BBC before developing it into a book for Chatto and Windus. He epitomises a particular kind of modern, ambitious academic, who peddles his work to further his career, without any real feeling for his vocation.

The fiction of the poem is built up by precise reference. The young man is indulging in reflections aboard his Comet during a flight from London to Bombay on Armistice Day:

> Crowds, colourless and careworn,
> Had made my taxi late,

> Yet not till I was airborne
> Did I recall the date –
> That day when Queen and Minister
> And Band of Guards and all
> Still act their solemn-sinister
> Wreath-rubbish in Whitehall.

Devoid of compassion for the families of the war dead, he feels only irritation with the crowds who have delayed him. That these attitudes are not shared by Larkin is evidenced by his profound feelings about the terrible changes wrought in people's lives and in the life of the nation by the First World War in 'MCMXIV'. In 'Naturally the Foundation will Bear Your Expenses' Larkin chooses to promote his own point of view by encouraging the reader to react against the speaker, who is condemned out of his own mouth. To this end he provides for the academic a recognisably personal language composed of bitingly contemptuous but rather adolescent wit. He evinces a supercilious attitude to simple human emotions such as patriotism, and his system of values is readily identified as including physical ease, wealth, fame and second-hand contact through his 'pal' with famous literary figures such as 'Morgan Forster'. Egocentric, smug and callous, he has reneged on those values traditionally associated with scholarship and humane studies: passion for truth, reverence for the past, and a love of humanity.

Embarrassment and indignation also control the form of a similar but more complex dramatic monologue, 'Posterity', from *High Windows*, in which Larkin satirises the perverted values of a young American university teacher, who is desperate to obtain tenure by finishing his PhD thesis or publishing a book. This is both a subtler and more humorous poem because Larkin, with a fine sense of the absurd, immediately introduces himself: 'Jake Balokowsky, my biographer, / Has this page microfilmed'. This at once sets up a tension between the *persona*, the poet and the reader. While on the one hand this device angles the monologue towards fiction, establishing the autonomy of the speaker's world, on the other it undercuts our sense of the truth of the fiction by alerting us to the controlling presence of the poet himself. Tension is further heightened by a combination within the reader of a growing antagonism towards the speaker, and a simultaneous sense of acute embarrassment, and therefore a measure of sympathy, as he is forced to eavesdrop on the speaker's judgement of the poet whose company we share.

The pun in the academic's name and the comic futility of his having microfilmed a page that is still in print, or even perhaps is still being written, encapsulates Larkin's opinion of him as a bogus scholar, interested in research only in so far as it provides him with material security. Larkin establishes the fictional reality of his speaker in his own often coarse language, which registers among other things his embarrassment at his choice of research topic:

> It's stinking dead, the research line;
> Just let me put this bastard on the skids,
> I'll get a couple of semesters leave
>
> To work on Protest Theater.

Ironically he perverts those very values that his chosen profession represents. Far from writing on a poet whom he understands and admires, he is working on the life of a man he despises for his boring life and old-fashioned beliefs:

> What's he like?
> Christ, I just told you. Oh, you know the thing,
> That crummy textbook stuff from Freshman Psych,
> Not out of kicks or something happening –
> One of those old-type *natural* fouled-up guys.

Larkin's marvellous ear for idiom and speech rhythms captures the young man's boredom and irritation, for at the back of his mind are the ever-present claims of his wife, his parents-in-law and his children. However, although he is arrogant, greedy and indifferent to both literary and human values, his judgement of the poet is allowed to make a neat counterpoint to the poet's oblique judgement of him. Larkin does not merely permit the speaker to condemn himself, but he also employs his alien point of view to place the poet's own writing in a wider perspective. For all its ignorance and venom, the academic's description of the poet implies that there are significant limitations in his poetry. And the reader is also alerted to significant parallels between the academic and the poet – the similar disappointments, the tension between romantic longing and a necessary pragmatism, for instance. Except that – and this is the central irony in Larkin's elaborate joke – we have the poem itself. The reader is left to judge from this serious yet witty poem just how 'old-type' and 'fouled-up' the poet really is, and which of the two, the poet or his critic, comes off worse. By using the form of the dramatic monologue to gain distance, and by utilising the reader's own embarrassment to obtain a measure of sympathy for the odious speaker, Larkin deals tactfully and humorously with the difficult and embarrassing task of facing the incomprehension and negative judgement of some of his critics.

One criticism that has been made of Larkin is precisely this air of detachment that some readers find in his poetry. And it is certainly true that the speaker in many of his poems, such as 'Church Going', is something of an isolate. The speaker in 'Sympathy in White Major', from *High Windows*, has chosen the solitary life as a way of preserving for others the significance of their own intense activity, though, as he confesses, 'It didn't work for them or me.' And the speaker in 'Here', from *The Whitsun Weddings*, states a preference for 'Isolate villages, where removed lives / Loneliness clarifies'. And in 'Vers de Société', from *High Windows*, there is the expression of a desire to avoid society. But this quality of isolation in many of Larkin's *personae* does not denote withdrawal. For instance, in the poem 'High Windows' the nature of solitary being does not preclude imaginative involvement with the world, though this is won at the cost of some embarrassment. Here the speaker's voice is close to Larkin's own, but the language defines what aspect of Larkin is implied. The word 'fucking' is a consciously brutal way of covering up the speaker's envy of the young lovers, which helps to develop his personality.

The *persona*'s keen awareness of the physical and social world,

in this case his observation of a 'couple of kids', leads naturally
to his reflection about the quality of their evident liberation from
the sexual inhibitions and anxieties of the speaker's youth, and
he gives his assent to the new values in a relaxed, colloquial tone.
But this apparent complacency in fact conceals an embarrassment
and an angry frustration at the way the past limits the present.
Like the *persona* in 'Send No Money', he is disillusioned by life
and disappointed that his youthful hope of happiness has come
to nothing. As Andrew Motion has pointed out,[22] his speech
modulates from ironical grumbling to a symbolist intensity when
he considers how his elders in their turn had envied his freedom:

> And immediately

> Rather than words comes the thought of high windows:
> The sun-comprehending glass,
> And beyond it, the deep blue air, that shows
> Nothing, and is nowhere, and is endless.

This moment of epiphany offers a kind of transcendence, but the
sort of freedom it presents as an alternative to the secular and
sexual liberation of the young couple is qualified by the fact that
it is also neutral vacancy. Yet clearly the 'long slide / To happiness'
is a reductive, disillusioning process, which is counterpointed by
the elevation to the vision of high windows. In this poem the
persona's mask gradually crumbles away to reveal, beneath the
embarrassment, the boredom and the anger, an impulse of
affirmation, ambivalently felt, and beyond words.

There are several dramatic monologues among Larkin's writing
to date in which the *persona* is much closer to the poet's own voice,
and which reveal different facets of his poetic personality. In
'Reasons for Attendance', from *The Less Deceived*, Larkin creates
a *persona* close to that of his role of an academic librarian, thus
presenting a slant view of his opinions from an area of his
experience that derives from his professional role. The speaker
has probably been invited to a student dance (the title implies
something like this). He feels profoundly embarrassed and employs
his dry wit to intellectualise his situation and keep emotion safely

at bay. He denies that he is lured to the window of the dance hall by anything other than the sound of the trumpet: 'that lifted, rough-tongued bell / (Art, if you like)', and certainly not by the 'maul to and fro' of the dancers. The call of the trumpet and the sight of the couples dancing lead the speaker to speculate rather pompously about the nature of happiness. Just as art – in this case the individual note of the trumpet – seems to insist on the speaker's individuality, so too he feels that happiness is to be found in solitude rather than in couples. However, the speaker unwillingly betrays his true feelings when he talks lasciviously about the 'wonderful feel of girls', and when he protests complacently about the assumption that

> the lion's share
> Of happiness is found by couples – sheer
>
> Inaccuracy, as far as I'm concerned.

His strident insistence that happiness resides in art and solitude rather than in life and sexuality conceals a very real fear of loneliness and of having missed the secret of happiness altogether. Nevertheless, the speaker is well aware of the defensive game he is playing. This is signalled to the reader in the smug jingle of the parallelism in the final stanza:

> Therefore I stay outside,
> Believing this; and they maul to and fro,
> Believing that; and both are satisfied

– at which point the speaker feels compelled to drop his mask and add with wry bitterness, 'If no one has misjudged himself. Or lied.' The effectiveness of this poem thus depends on Larkin's use of the formal mask, which is nevertheless quite close to the poet's personality; on the tension between the confessional impulse and the embarrassed, defensive posture; on the subtle modulations of tone, and on the ruthless honesty with which the speaker turns the irony upon himself.

Larkin's gift for dramatising the workings of his speakers' minds is perhaps best exemplified in 'Dockery and Son', from *The*

Whitsun Weddings, in which the *persona* is very close to the situation of the poet himself, but in which the identification is not made explicit, in order to give full play to the flux and reflux of the speaker's mind. The eight-line stanza and the simple rhyme scheme permit shifts of tone and modulations of thought and feeling as he reflects on his visit to his former college, where he has discovered with a shock how differently from his own the lives of his contemporaries have developed. The most forceful contrast is between his own, childless, solitary existence and that of Dockery, whose son is now in college:

> Dockery, now:
> Only nineteen, he must have taken stock
> Of what he wanted, and been capable
> Of . . . No, that's not the difference: rather, how
> Convinced he was he should be added to!

The poem moves through the speaker's consideration of the 'ranged / Joining and parting lines' in the moonlight at Sheffield station, which creates a metaphor for his life and those of his fellow students such as Dockery, and Larkin conveys exactly the play of his mind:

> Where do these
> Innate assumptions come from? Not from what
> We think truest, or most want to do:
> Those warp tight-shut, like doors. They're more a style
> Our lives bring with them: habit for a while,
> Suddenly they harden into all we've got
>
> And how we got it; looked back on, they rear
> Like sand-clouds, thick and close, embodying
> For Dockery a son, for me nothing,
> Nothing with all a son's harsh patronage.

The speaker gropes his way towards the final bleak statement, which is delivered in the concluding stanza, where the comforting regularity of the iambic pentameter is replaced by the curt, menacing

Life is first boredom, then fear.
Whether or not we use it, it goes,
And leaves what something hidden from us chose,
And age, and then the only end of age.

Here as in many of Larkin's poems, the speaker is embarrassed,
thwarted by the past, frustrated by missed opportunities that
nevertheless overshadow the future, but above all by the mysterious
nature of the process which renders this inevitable.

Finally an important area of experience which Larkin explores
through the dramatic monologue is the way in which embarrassment forces people to assume social masks. 'Vers de Société', from
High Windows, which is once more very close to the poet's own
voice, is concerned with the running conflict between the speaker's
preference for solitude and society's demand for intercourse. The
poem opens with the speaker's ironic reinterpretation of the true
sentiments that lie behind a formal invitation to a party that he
knows he will hate:

> *My wife and I have asked a crowd of craps*
> *To come and waste their time and ours: perhaps*
> *You'd care to join us?*

And it closes with his own conventional lie framed in polite reply:
'*Dear Warlock-Williams: Why, of course* –'. The comedy lies in the
fact that neither host nor guest really wants the party to take
place, and the speaker's immediate, honest response to the
invitation is a brutal sneer: 'In a pig's arse, friend.' The poem
records his attempt to explore the reasons for his embarrassed,
intemperate reaction. He notes how the claims that society makes
on the individual grow harder to resist as he gets older, and,
although he is bitingly satirical about those awful parties where
he has to listen to 'some bitch / Who's read nothing but *Which*',
ask 'that ass about his fool research', and fill his evenings with
'forks and faces' instead of reading in the company of wind and
moon, he also poignantly evokes the darkening evening and the
closing in of life: 'Day comes to an end. / The gas fire breathes,
the trees are darkly swayed.' In fact the speaker's attack on party-
going is less harsh than it seems, for it is clear from the poem that

his sour comments emerge not from any settled, smug conviction of intellectual or moral superiority, but from acute feelings of fear and failure. He suggests that, because such gatherings represent, however imperfectly, a human ideal, solitude may be regarded in a fundamental sense as anti-social. But he finds this moral tone even more embarrassing than his anger, because in truth for him as for so many other people, his hosts included, social intercourse is a means of escaping for a while the dreadful pangs of remorse and despair, and the painful acknowledgement of the encroachment of time. The monologue brilliantly traces the movement of the speaker's mind from an instinctively hostile rejection of society's impertinent claims, to a reluctant decision to reconstruct his social mask, a process which ironically inverts the cliché '*All solitude is selfish*' through the realisation, both savage and compassionate, that society represents a profound need for human solidarity, of which the party is a poignant if ambiguous symbol.

Like those poets he most admires, Larkin employs traditional forms such as the dramatic monologue in order primarily to serve the content of his poetry, and to communicate vividly and memorably with the reader. His use of *personae* in these poems I have been discussing belies the critical orthodoxy that his writing is deeply pessimistic and limited in scope. His *personae* are very different; they may be witty, tender, callous, morosely self-regarding, aesthetically stunted or refined, or inclined to mysticism – Larkin's view of life is located in no single *persona* or poem, for each reflects only one facet of a poetic personality that is remarkably versatile.

At the heart of his poetry, as in the poetry of Wordsworth, Hardy and Betjeman, is the relation between the physical world and the world of the human spirit; between the environments within which we live and our capacity for love and growth. Larkin has an extraordinarily developed ability to register precisely detailed observation, but in his poetry, as in Betjeman's, 'the eye leads the spirit',[23] and the characteristic development of his dramatic monologues is from an initial, intensely visualised scene through a commentary which moves tentatively but with inexorable logic towards a difficult and honest assessment of experience. The reader is always aware of being in the presence of a delicate sensibility and a penetrating intelligence; of entering a poetic world informed by both compassion and wit. The simultaneous engagement of Larkin's romantic sensibility and his almost classical restraint and discipline accounts for the tension in his poetry between the impulse towards symbolist moments of epiphany and transcendence, and a rigorous scepticism embodied in the careful logic of his syntax.

This is the centre of Larkin's moral realism. He is open to both suffering and joy, and like Hardy he regards suffering as an essentially maturing experience, leading in Hardy's phrase to 'the soul's betterment'.[24] Unlike Modernism, which, as Larkin has said, 'whether perpetrated by Parker, Pound or Picasso . . . helps us neither to enjoy nor endure',[25] Larkin's poetry is fundamentally concerned to do both. And one potent means of achieving this is the particular rhetoric that he employs in those poems I have been discussing, the medium of shared embarrassment, which develops in the reader a profounder sense of his humanity. This 'fundamental nexus between poet and audience' is, as Larkin has testified, the basis of his poetic art.[26] He has opened up in a unique and important way new channels of communication between contemporary poetry and the reading public; and in doing so he carries forward the Romantic reinterpretation of the English tradition of poetry of equipoise.

Notes

CHAPTER 1: POETRY OF EQUIPOISE: TRADITION IN MODERN VERSE

1. Geoffrey Thurley, *The Ironic Harvest* (London, 1974) p. 1.

2. See Donald Davie, *Purity of Diction in English Verse* (London, 1967).

3. Yvor Winters, 'The Plain Style Reborn', in *Forms of Discovery* (Chicago, 1967).

4. William Empson, *Seven Types of Ambiguity* (London, 1930) pp. 20–1.

5. F. R. Leavis, *New Bearings in English Poetry* (London, 1932).

6. Thurley, *The Ironic Harvest*, p. 19.

7. Ibid.

8. Donald Davie, 'On Sincerity', *Encounter*, Oct 1968, quoted in Thurley, *The Ironic Harvest*, p. 3.

9. Andrew Motion, 'On the Plain of Holderness', in *Larkin at Sixty*, ed. Anthony Thwaite (London, 1982) p. 66.

10. Philip Larkin, 'A Great Parade of Single Poems: Interview with Anthony Thwaite', *Listener*, 12 Apr 1973, p. 473.

11. John Wain (ed.), *Selected Shorter Poems of Thomas Hardy* (London, 1966) p. xi.

12. C. K. Stead, *The New Poetic* (London, 1964, repr. 1975) pp. 11–12.

13. William Wordsworth, Preface to *Lyrical Ballads*, ed. R. L. Brett and A. R. Jones (London, 1963, repr. 1978) pp. 255–6, 247, 251.

14. John Press, *Rule and Energy* (London, 1963) p. 102.

15. Terry Whalen, 'Philip Larkin's Imagist Bias: His Poetry of Observation', *Critical Quarterly*, 23 (1981) 45.

16. Philip Larkin, Introduction to 'Faith Healing', on the Marvell Press recording *Philip Larkin Reads and Comments on 'The Whitsun Weddings'*, Listen Records LPV 6 (1965).

17. Wordsworth, Preface to *Lyrical Ballads*, p. 247.

18. Philip Larkin, 'It Could Only Happen in England', in *Required Writing* (London, 1983) p. 209.

19. David Timms, *Philip Larkin* (Edinburgh, 1973) p. 62.

20. Philip Larkin, 'The Pleasure Principle', in *Required Writing*, p. 82.

21. Wordsworth, Preface to *Lyrical Ballads*, p. 251.

22. Thomas Hardy, in *Thomas Hardy's Personal Writings*, ed. Harold Orel (London, 1967) p. 52.

23. Philip Larkin, 'Wanted: Good Hardy Critic', *Critical Quarterly*, 8 (1966) 178.

24. Donald Davie, *Thomas Hardy and British Poetry* (London, 1973) pp. 63–82.

25. Philip Larkin, 'The Poetry of Thomas Hardy', in *Required Writing*, p. 175.

26. Timms, *Philip Larkin*, p. 58.

27. Blake Morrison, *The Movement* (London, 1980) p. 231. Morrison also finds a possible influence in Betjeman's 'Sunday Afternoon Service in St Enodoc Church, Cornwall' (p. 232).

28. Davie, *Thomas Hardy and British Poetry*, pp. 108–10.

29. Philip Larkin, 'The Blending of Betjeman', in *Required Writing*, p. 132.

30. Philip Larkin, Introduction to *John Betjeman: Collected Poems* (London, 1971) p. xxiii.

31. Larkin, 'It Could Only Happen in England', in *Required Writing*, p. 211.

32. Timms, *Philip Larkin*, pp. 117–18.

33. Larkin, 'It Could Only Happen in England', in *Required Writing*, p. 217.

34. Davie, *Thomas Hardy and British Poetry*, p. 64.

35. Quoted in Patrick Taylor-Martin, *John Betjeman* (London, 1983) p. 76.

36. Larkin, in *Poets of the 1950s*, ed. D. J. Enright (Tokyo, 1955) pp. 77–8.

37. Graham Hough, *Image and Experience* (London, 1960) p. 40.

38. Neil Powell, *Carpenters of Light* (Manchester, 1979) p. 7.

39. T. S. Eliot, in the *Athenaeum*, 9 May 1919, quoted in C. K. Stead, *The New Poetic*, p. 109.

40. Larkin, 'The Pleasure Principle', in *Required Writing*, pp. 81–2.

41. Philip Larkin, 'No Fun Anymore', *Manchester Guardian*, 18 Nov 1958, p. 4.

42. Larkin, 'It Could Only Happen in England', in *Required Writing*, p. 209.

43. Ian Hamilton, 'Four Conversations: Philip Larkin', *London Magazine*, Nov 1964, pp. 71–2.

CHAPTER 2: WILLIAM WORDSWORTH: RATIONAL SYMPATHY

1. Wordsworth, Preface to *Lyrical Ballads*, p. 247.

2. Ibid., pp. 245–6.

3. Ibid., p. 256.

4. Ibid., p. 258.

5. Ibid., p. 266.

6. Ibid., pp. 245–6.

7. Ibid., p. 246.

8. Ibid., p. 265.

9. Ibid., p. 247.

10. Ibid., p. 261.

11. See Angus Easson, ' "The Idiot Boy": Wordsworth Serves out his Poetic Indentures', *Critical Quarterly*, 22 (1980) 3–18.

12. *Letters of William and Dorothy Wordsworth: The Early Years 1787–1805*, ed. Ernest de Selincourt, 2nd edn, rev. Chester L. Shaver (Oxford, 1967) p. 357.

13. Wordsworth, Preface to *Lyrical Ballads*, p. 261.

14. Ibid., pp. 255–6.

15. Yvor Winters, *Forms of Discovery* (Chicago, 1967) pp. 167–8.

16. *Wordsworth's Poetical Works*, ed. E. de Selincourt and Helen Darbishire (Oxford, 1946) III, 431.

17. Wordsworth, Preface to *Lyrical Ballads*, p. 249.

18. *Wordsworth's Poetical Works*, III, 431.

19. Ibid., III, 424.

CHAPTER 3: THOMAS HARDY: MOMENTS OF VISION

1. Thurley, *The Ironic Harvest* (London, 1974) p. 32.

2. Ibid., p. 34.

3. Tom Paulin, *Thomas Hardy: The Poetry of Perception* (London, 1975) p. 36.

4. Paul Zietlow, *Moments of Vision: The Poetry of Thomas Hardy* (Cambridge, Mass., 1974) p. 10.

5. As early as 1868 Hardy had proposed to write a volume of poems on this subject. See Florence Emily Hardy, *The Life of Thomas Hardy 1840–1928* (London, 1962) p. 58.

6. Wordsworth, Preface to *Lyrical Ballads*, p. 247.

7. Florence Emily Hardy, *The Life of Thomas Hardy*, p. 114.

8. Ibid., p. 185.

9. Ibid., p. 415.

10. Samuel Taylor Coleridge, *Biographia Literaria*, ed. George Watson (London, 1956) p. 173.

11. J. Hillis Miller, *Thomas Hardy: Distance and Desire* (Cambridge, Mass., 1970) p. 22.

12. Thomas Hardy, 'Apology' to *Late Lyrics and Earlier*, in *Thomas Hardy's Personal Writings*, p. 53.

13. Hillis Miller, *Thomas Hardy: Distance and Desire*, p. 4

14. Hardy, in *Thomas Hardy's Personal Writings*, p. 52.

15. Davie, *Thomas Hardy and British Poetry*, p. 28.

16. Paulin, *Thomas Hardy: The Poetry of Perception*, p. 138.

17. See *Some Recollections by Emma Hardy*, ed. Evelyn Hardy and Robert Gittings (London, 1961) p. 5.

CHAPTER 4: JOHN BETJEMAN: AN ODEON FLASHES FIRE

1. Quoted in Patrick Taylor-Martin, *John Betjeman* (London, 1983) p. 13.

2. Press, *Rule and Energy*, p. 7.

3. Larkin, 'The Blending of Betjeman', in *Required Writing*, p. 129.

4. Taylor-Martin, *John Betjeman*, p. 179.

5. Davie, *Thomas Hardy and British Poetry*, p. 108.

6. Quoted in Taylor-Martin, *John Betjeman*, p. 76.

7. Betjeman offers a satirical revised version of 'The New Bath Guide' (1766), by Christopher Anstey, a poem celebrating the civilised amenities of eighteenth-century Bath.

8. Larkin, 'It Could Only Happen in England', in *Required Writing*, p. 211.

9. Ibid., p. 217.

CHAPTER 5: PHILIP LARKIN: REASONS FOR ATTENDANCE

1. Larkin, 'It Could Only Happen in England', in *Required Writing*, p. 217.

2. Philip Larkin, 'Subsidizing Poetry', ibid., p. 92.

3. For a stimulating discussion of this theme see Christopher Ricks, *Keats and Embarrassment* (Oxford, 1974).

4. Anon., 'Speaking of Writing XIII: Philip Larkin', *The Times*, 20 Feb 1964, p. 16.

5. Larkin, 'The Pleasure Principle', in *Required Writing*, pp. 81–2.

6. Christopher Ricks, 'Like Something Almost Being Said', in *Larkin at Sixty*, ed. Thwaite, p. 123.

7. Hamilton, 'Four Conversations: Philip Larkin', *London Magazine*, Nov 1964, p. 73.

8. Press, *Rule and Energy* (London, 1963) p. 105.

9. Larkin, in *Poets of the 1950s*, ed. D. J. Enright, p. 77.

10. Larkin, in *The Observer*, 16 Dec 1979, p. 35.

11. Andrew Motion, *Philip Larkin* (London, 1982).

12. Charles Tomlinson, 'Poetry Today', in *The Pelican Guide to English Literature* VII: *The Modern Age*, ed. Boris Ford, 2nd edn (Harmondsworth, 1964) p. 459.

13. Larkin, 'Not Like Larkin' (transcription from BBC Radio 3), *Listener*, 88 (1972) 209.

14. Larkin, 'The Pleasure Principle', in *Required Writing*, p. 82.

15. Hamilton, 'Four Conversations: Philip Larkin', *London Magazine*, Nov 1964, pp. 74–5.

16. Ibid., p. 74.

17. Powell, *Carpenters of Light*, p. 86.

18. Clive James, 'Don Juan in Hull', in *At the Pillars of Hercules* (London, 1979) p. 54.

19. John Wain, letter to the *London Magazine*, Mar 1957, p. 56.

20. John Press, 'English Verse since 1945', in *Essays by Divers Hands*, XXXI, ed. Peter Green (London, 1962) p. 169.

21. Hamilton, 'Four Conversations: Philip Larkin', *London Magazine*, Nov 1964, p. 76.

22. Motion, *Philip Larkin*, p. 81.

23. Larkin, Introduction to *John Betjeman: Collected Poems*, p. xxiii.

24. Hardy, in *Thomas Hardy's Personal Writings*, p. 52.

25. Philip Larkin, Introduction to *All What Jazz*, in *Required Writing*, p. 297.

26. Larkin, 'Subsidizing Poetry', in *Required Writing*, p. 92.

Select Bibliography

This is primarily a selected list of those works which I have found most useful in writing this study.

Abrams, M. H., *The Mirror and the Lamp: Romantic Theory and the Critical Tradition* (New York, 1953).

Bailey, James O., *The Poetry of Thomas Hardy* (Chapel Hill, NC, 1970).

Bayley, John, 'Larkin and the Romantic Tradition', *Critical Quarterly*, 26 (1984) 61–6.

Brooks, Cleanth, *Modern Poetry and the Tradition* (Chapel Hill, NC, 1939).

Coleridge, Samuel Taylor, *Biographia Literaria*, ed. George Watson (London, 1956).

Davie, Donald, *Articulate Energy: An Inquiry into the Syntax of English Poetry* (London, 1955).

——, *Purity of Diction in English Verse* (London, 1952).

——, *Thomas Hardy and British Poetry* (London, 1973).

Dyson, A. E., 'Symbiosis in Wordsworth', *Critical Survey*, 6 (1973) 41–3.

Easson, Angus, ' "The Idiot Boy": Wordsworth Serves out his Poetic Indentures', *Critical Quarterly*, 22 (1980) 3–18.

Empson, William, *Seven Types of Ambiguity* (London, 1930).

Enright, D. J. (ed.), *Poets of the 1950s* (Tokyo, 1955).

Everett, Barbara, 'Philip Larkin: After Symbolism', *Essays in Criticism*, 30 (1980) 227–42.

Hamburger, Michael, *The Truth of Poetry: Tensions in Modern Poetry from Baudelaire to the 1960s* (London, 1969).

Hamilton, Ian, 'Four Conversations: Philip Larkin', *London Magazine* (Nov 1964) 71–82.

Hardy, Thomas, *The Complete Poems of Thomas Hardy*, Variorum Edition, ed. James Gibson (London, 1979).

Hardy, Thomas, *Thomas Hardy's Personal Writings*, ed. Harold Orel (London, 1967).

Hartman, Geoffrey, *Wordsworth's Poetry, 1787–1814* (New Haven, Conn., and London, 1964).

Hough, Graham, *Image and Experience* (London, 1960).

Hynes, Samuel, *The Pattern of Hardy's Poetry* (Chapel Hill, NC, 1961).

131

James, Clive, *At the Pillars of Hercules* (London, 1979).

Langbaum, Robert, *The Poetry of Experience: The Dramatic Monologue in Modern Literary Tradition* (Harmondsworth, 1974).

Larkin, Philip, *Required Writing* (London, 1983).

Leavis, F. R., *New Bearings in English Poetry* (London, 1932).

——, *Revaluation: Tradition and Development in English Poetry* (London, 1936).

Miller, J. Hillis, *Thomas Hardy: Distance and Desire* (Cambridge, Mass., 1970).

Morrison, Blake, *The Movement* (London, 1980).

Motion, Andrew, *Philip Larkin* (London, 1982).

Parrish, Stephen Maxfield, *The Art of the 'Lyrical Ballads'* (Cambridge, Mass., 1973).

Paulin, Tom, *Thomas Hardy: The Poetry of Perception* (London, 1975).

Powell, Neil, *Carpenters of Light* (Manchester, 1979).

Press, John, *John Betjeman*, Writers and their Work (London, 1974).

——, *Rule and Energy* (London, 1963).

Ricks, Christopher, *Keats and Embarrassment* (Oxford, 1974).

Simpson, David, *Irony and Authority in Romantic Poetry* (London, 1979).

Sinfield, Alan, *Dramatic Monologue* (London, 1977).

Stanford, Derek, *John Betjeman: A Study* (London, 1961).

Stead, C. K., *The New Poetic* (London, 1964).

Taylor, Dennis, *Hardy's Poetry 1860–1928* (London, 1981).

Taylor-Martin, Patrick, *John Betjeman: His Life and Work* (London, 1983).

Thurley, Geoffrey, *The Ironic Harvest: English Poetry in the Twentieth Century* (London, 1974).

Thwaite, Anthony (ed.), *Larkin at Sixty* (London, 1982).

Timms, David, *Philip Larkin* (Edinburgh, 1973).

Wain, John, *Essays on Literature and Ideas* (London, 1963).

Whalen, Terry, 'Philip Larkin's Imagist Bias: His Poetry of Observation', *Critical Quarterly*, 23 (1981) 29–46.

Winters, Yvor, *Forms of Discovery* (Chicago, 1967).

Wordsworth, William, *The Poetical Works of William Wordsworth*, ed. E. de Selincourt and Helen Darbishire, 5 vols (Oxford, 1940–9).

——, and Coleridge, Samuel Taylor, *Lyrical Ballads*, ed. R. L. Brett and A. R. Jones (London, 1963).

Zietlow, Paul, *Moments of Vision: The Poetry of Thomas Hardy* (Cambridge, Mass., 1974).

Index

133